John A. Andrews Jr.

PUTTING YOUR FAITH TO WORK

PUTTING YOUR
FAITH TO WORK

JOHN A. REDHEAD

ABINGDON PRESS

NEW YORK
NASHVILLE

PUTTING YOUR FAITH TO WORK

Copyright © MCMLIX by Abingdon Press

Library of Congress Catalog Card Number: 59-12784

SET UP, PRINTED, AND BOUND BY THE
PARTHENON PRESS, AT NASHVILLE,
TENNESSEE, UNITED STATES OF AMERICA

CONTENTS

5

How Can I Make
My Faith Work?

"Whatsoever things are true, . . . [keep on thinking] on these things."—*Phil. 4:8*

FOR SOME TIME THE IMPRESSION HAS BEEN GROWING UPON ME THAT most of our failures to make a practical success of Christian living come from not having a handle on our faith. Time and again I have sat down with some person who was conscious of such failure and who wanted to overcome it. Invariably he started off by saying the same thing which all the rest had said: "Now of course I've got faith, but—" He didn't finish the sentence but what he meant was this: "I've got faith but—my life is a mess!" On one hand, faith, on the other hand, the failure to make a practical success of Christian living.

Of course faith by itself never helped any man; it is what you do with the faith you have which makes the difference in your life. If you want your faith to work, then you have to work your faith; the reason more of us do not work our faith is that we do not know where to take hold of it. We are like the man who was so ignorant of the game of golf that he did not know which end of the caddie to take hold of. There is hardly anything which would mean more to us than to get a handle on our faith.

There is a word in Paul which is handmade for this purpose. He is writing to the Philippians, and he says in words with which you are quite familiar: "Finally, brethren, whatsoever things are true, whatsoever things are honest, whatsoever things are just," and so on, "think on these things." That is not exactly what he says. The form of the verb which he uses when he tells us to "think" says in effect: "keep on thinking." It is not simply a passing thought which you are to give to the kind of things.

7

suggested in the verse; it is rather a habit of mind which will keep on thinking on these things so constantly that there is no room in the mind for anything else. Whatsoever things are true and good, keep on thinking on these things.

Here is a handle which is in reach of every one of us, the control of the thoughts which occupy our minds. That may seem to be a small matter, and yet it is a fundamental truth about human nature that what gets your attention gets you. That is the reason you businessmen are willing to spend so much money in advertising. You know that what gets a man's attention gets him, and that if you can succeed in keeping a Ford or a Plymouth or a Chevrolet in the center of his attention long enough by means of the billboards and the newspapers, eventually you will get him. Whatsoever thing you can get a man to keep on thinking on, that thing will eventually control that man's life. Here is a handle we can take hold of, and it is our business now to see wherein it can make our faith work toward a practical success in Christian living.

I

Take it as it applies, first of all, in relation to that most common problem of fear and anxiety and worry. Those who have made a study of human nature tell us that Private Enemy Number One is fear. Any preacher knows that if he wants to choose a theme that will apply to all his listeners, he can always get it right here. Most of us are, at times, afraid of losing our health and anxious about our job or worried about what will happen to those whom we love. Because Jesus knew what was in human nature, he had a great deal to say about this particular emotion. Fear not, he tells us. Take no anxious thought about tomorrow. He was always talking about this problem because he knew it was an ever-present danger with people.

The truth is, you will find just about as much anxiety and worry in the minds of Christians as with those who claim no connection with Christ. I think of that woman who, though she was the daughter of a bishop and might have been expected to have a working faith, always grew frantic at the approach of a storm and gathered her children with her into the darkest closet she could find. Apparently there is no clear line to be drawn between Christians and non-Christians in their attitude toward superstition. One is just as much afraid of a black cat as another. Otherwise supposedly intelligent and religious persons will pay their money and put their trust in fortunetellers, as though God had resigned and turned things over to a clever fellow with a crystal ball. The truth is that if Jesus ever intended our faith to deliver us from our fears, he is greatly disappointed.

Yet that is our fault, not his. Our faith can deliver us from our fears, and here is a picture of the way it works. All of you remember the movie *Snow White and the Seven Dwarfs.* When it was advertised, all the mothers of young children thought it would be a good fairy story and so promised their boys and girls they could see it. But when it came, there was an old witch in it, and some thought such a horror picture might set up unwholesome fears in the minds of their children. Yet they had promised the boys and girls they might see the movie, and a promise with a child is a promise. The parents faced a dilemma. If the children saw the movie, it might have an ill effect; if they could not see it, the parents had broken a promise. So it was settled this way: the children were allowed to go to the theater, but just before the witch came on, they were taken out. That week a young friend of ours was playing with some older boys and remarked that he was going to see Snow White next day. These older boys, wanting to show their superiority, looked down their noses at him and told him he was so little he would have to get up and leave before the witch came on. "No, I'm not," he said; "I'm going with my daddy, and when the witch comes on, I'm not going to look at the witch; I'm just going to look at my daddy."

What wisdom that little mind possessed! He knew it to be true that he had a daddy and that no witch had the power to frighten him as long as he had his daddy with him. Whatsoever things are true then, keep on thinking on these things. Here is a handle to put on your faith. You know that God is your Father and that in his presence no fear has ground to stand on. Why then are you afraid? Because you are careless and yield the center of the stage to your fears instead of to your Father. From now on say this: "Whenever any witch comes on the screen of my mind, I am not going to look at the witch; I am going to look at my Father." It worked for the little boy, and it will work for you.

II

Move on now to the second place. Note how this handle can make our faith work in another area, the area of conscious inadequacy. A large majority of folk feel unequal to their responsibilities. Most people you meet will tell you they have so much to do these days they don't see how they will ever get it done. You go to bed at night and the only thing you can think of is the stack of duties a mile high to be tackled on the morrow and you do not see for the life of you how you can ever get through the day.

You say to yourself, I have power enough to lift only five pounds and must lift ten. As a consequence you grow weary with the constant round, feel all in, and before you know it, you are telling yourself that you just cannot go on.

The fact of which you are not conscious is that the way you

feel is largely a result of the way in which you have been talking to yourself. You say concerning a man who arrived at a certain decision: he talked himself into it. Well, many a person talks himself into a breakdown. The reason such a thing is possible is the way our minds work. There is a part of the mind which is below the level of consciousness, and it is like a factory. It takes the raw material which you feed it in the form of thoughts, and out of this raw material it manufactures the finished product. Because of the defeatist words and debilitating thoughts which we feed into our factory, the product is too often finished, done for, all in.

If it is possible for a man to talk himself into a breakdown, it is also possible for him to talk himself into a build-up, if his talk is not just talk but has behind it the truth of reality.

That is where our faith comes in. Paul says, "I can do all things through him who strengthens me. I do not have to pull this power out of thin air. I can because God can." Notice the difference between the apostle and ourselves. We approach any task in the negative. We say, I just know I can't do it. Paul talks to himself more encouragingly. He says, I can.

If you will take a cue from the apostle, you will discover that his method pays off. Before you go to sleep at night, instead of saying, "I have power to lift only five pounds and must lift ten," say rather, "I have power to lift ten pounds and need lift only five." Instead of saying, "I have so much to do tomorrow I don't see how I will ever get through," say rather, "I have many things ahead of me, and it will take a great deal of strength to get through the day, but God and I are more than a match for anything that turns up."

Here is a handle for your faith. It is true, isn't it, that you and God are a winning team? Well, whatsoever things are true, keep

11

thinking on these things. Keep thinking on them by constantly setting them in the center of your attention. If for one week you will put this handle on your faith and by this means throw your religion into gear, you will find yourself taking all the hills in high.

III

Move on now into a third realm in which some of us are conscious of the need of help, the realm of temptation to wrongdoing.

The universality of the experience of temptation is too obvious to require elaboration. The majority of us would prefer being able to resist yielding to the wiles of the tempter. I know very few individuals who start out with a predetermined purpose to break God's laws, and are then proud of themselves for having succeeded. Most folks want to do what is right, and they profess a religion which claims to help a man do what is right, and yet many of us end by doing what is wrong. Why? Because we lack a handle which gives us a place to take hold of our faith and put it to work.

We can begin to fashion such a handle by noting that the origin of every sin is in the mind. Long ago a wise man named Augustine wrote the biography of sin in four words: a thought, a form, a fascination, a fall. First of all, a thought. You say no man alive can keep thoughts of evil from entering his mind, and that is true; but he can refuse to offer them hospitality. You can't keep the birds from flying over your head, but you can keep them from building nests in your hair. It is only when you offer such hospitality that the imagination will take a thought and give it form, and as you keep on thinking on that form, it acquires a certain fascination, and when one has gone that far, the fascination will almost inevitably lead to a fall.

Almost our only hope in overcoming temptation is in getting rid of the thought of evil when it presents itself. But right here is where most of us fall in the ditch: you cannot get rid of a thought simply by telling yourself to do so. The more you try not to think of a certain thing, the more certain you are to keep on thinking about it; and the more constantly you hold it in the center of attention, the more likely it is to get you. A man of magic offered to sell the secret of making gold to the natives in an African village. With a stick he stirred a pot of boiling water and, unseen to the others, let a few gold nuggets slip down the hollow stick. When they poured off the water, there was the gold. They paid him dearly for the secret: do as he had done, he told them, but be sure while they were stirring not to think of a green-eyed monkey. Try not to think of a green-eyed monkey and you cannot do so to save your life. The only way in the world to get rid of a thought is to put another in its place.

Time and again people have put me on the spot with the question as to how a man's religion can help at the place where he needs help, in the hour of temptation, and I have been forced to try to find an answer.

I remember one man sitting down in my study and saying, "I am a Christian, but I drink. I want to stop drinking, and I can't. What help can I expect from my religion to do what I want to do?"

I said, "The core of our religion is Christ. Do you believe in him?"

He said, "Yes."

I said, "Do you believe that he told the truth?"

He said, "Yes."

I said, "Do you believe Jesus told the truth when he said he would be with us till the end of time?"

He said, "Yes."

I said, "Do you believe Jesus is here in this room tonight in the presence of his Spirit?"

He said, "Yes."

I said, "If you believe, as you say you do, that it is wrong for you to drink liquor; and if you believe, as you say you do, that Jesus is here and that if we were not so blind we might see him sitting in that chair, could you take a drink where you are?"

And he said, "Not to save my life."

"Well," I said, "if that be true, the fault is ours and not our Lord's when our religion fails us."

The fault is ours, that we do not take hold of this handle. You can never get rid of a thought by trying not to think of it; you can rid yourself of it only by putting another in its place. It is true, is it not, that Jesus met the devil once in the wilderness and the devil ran up the white flag, and ever since he has been afraid to show his face when our Lord is around. That fact is true. Well and good. Whatsoever things are true, keep on thinking on these things. Here is a faith that will win, and here is a handle to make the faith work. The matter is squarely up to you and me as to whether we are willing to reach out and take hold of the handle.

I beseech you, brethren, by the mercies of God, take this handle and fasten it to your faith. Whatsoever things are true and good, keep on thinking on these things. What gets your attention gets you, and you have the say as to what gets your attention. I dare you in the name of all that's holy: fix your eyes upon your Saviour, look ever to Jesus, and then do anything of which you or he would be ashamed, if you can!

Where Can I Get
What I Want Most?

"He will fulfil the desire of them that fear him."—*Ps. 145:19*

SOME TIME AGO WHILE READING A BOOK ON HUMAN NATURE I HAP-
pened on this sentence: "Of the three major figures in modern
psychiatry, Freud may roughly be represented as saying that man
wants most of all to be loved; Jung that he wants most of all to
feel secure; Adler that he wants most of all to feel significant."
I went back and underscored those words, and the more I looked
at them the more I came to feel that they have something to say
to us.

They take note of the fact that most people want certain things.
They do not tell us what we ought to want; they tell us what we
do want. They suggest the difference between people is not so
much in what they want, as the way in which they seek to fulfill their wants.

The psalmist had never heard of Freud or Jung or Adler, but
he knew human nature and he knew God. He knew that what a
man wants most of all can be found in God. The Lord, he said,
"will fulfil the desire of them that fear him." We want to take
the words of these modern men of science and the words of this
ancient man of God and put them together; when de do, we
see that the basic needs of human nature find their answer in a
vital religious experience.

I

Let us begin with Mr. Adler. Since the discovery of the deep
mind, this thing called human nature has been laid bare before
the eyes of all who wished to study it. Mr. Adler took his turn
and came up with the report that when you get behind the scenes

15

and go right down to rock bottom, what a man wants most of all is to be somebody—to feel important, to be significant.

When you take an honest look at life you must admit that whether this deep desire to be somebody is what men want most, it is certainly something they do want. Watch a child on his birthday. He thoroughly enjoys it, and the reason is not far to seek. It is *his* day, he is the center of attention, and it makes him feel important. When that child grows up and becomes a man, he takes this same desire with him. I was never much of a football player on the field, but in my dreams I was a triple threat. I can remember dreaming that one day I took the ball on the kickoff, threaded my way through a broken field, and crossed the goal line as the crowds in the stands rose to their feet. If I could not secure a sense of significance in one way, then I would seek another; and the reason I am not ashamed to admit it is that I know you have had the same sort of dreams. This is the reason you always enjoy seeing your name in print. I had a letter from a newspaper clipping service in New York one day telling me that if I would send twenty-five cents I would receive an article with my name in it. I thought more of my quarter; but it interested me that such a service could stay in business. A man selling flowers walked the streets morning and afternoon with no success. Then he had an idea. He printed a sign and hung it on his basket: "Wear a red rose and feel important," and in ten minutes he had sold out.

Now the question is not whether we ought or ought not to have this desire; the fact is that we do have it, and the real issue is how we shall seek to fulfill it. Some men set out to make money because being rich makes one matter more. Some want to succeed because success makes them feel important. If they cannot achieve it any other way they invent strange methods: some dress to attract attention, some break all records eating hamburgers or drinking beer, some even become criminals because that is the only way to achieve eminence, and as a last resort some become insane and imagine themselves Napoleon. All of these habits are, at bottom, various ways of fulfilling that very human desire to feel important. And all the while the true answer is right here in our religion. The Lord, says the psalmist, "will fulfil the desire of them that fear him." And down across the years he has been doing just that.

For centuries kings and popes had things their own way, lording it over the common people with absolute power. Then men like Martin Luther and John Calvin began reading their Bibles and they came up with the idea that man is a child of God. They began talking about the dignity of the individual, and democracy was born. A friend of mine, a student in a theological school in downtown Louisville, told me of one of his professors who was in his dotage. The old gentleman started across the street, and when he saw an automobile coming, he held out his hand and said, "Stop, sir, and let me pass, for I am a prince, a son of the king of heaven." In like manner, this religious idea of the significance of the common man halted the traffic of absolute despotism, and then our world turned a corner into the modern era of freedom. Many a man, low in his mind and ready to throw himself away because he is not worth anything, has been picked up and set upon his feet, and sent on his way singing, "I am somebody because I am a child of God. I am of infinite worth in the eyes of the Infinite One who numbers the hairs of my head."

I talked one day with a man who had lost his self-respect. He had been a prisoner in the penitentiary, and the men from whom he sought employment did nothing to help his morale. I knew he would never be any good until he got back his faith in himself.

17

I remembered the way of Jesus with people, how he sat down by a well one day with a woman who did not think much of herself, and of how he sent her back believing in the possibility of being better tomorrow than she was yesterday; and so I said to him, "You have a right to believe in yourself because God still believes in you." He had not thought of it that way before; and when finally the truth of that good news began to dawn upon him, he walked out through the door with his shoulders back and his chin up. Even though he had touched bottom, as he thought, he felt within himself now the significance of new possibilities.

The first time I ever saw the Duke Chapel was during the Christmas holidays more than twenty years ago. With deep pride the unlettered caretaker showed us the beauties of the sanctuary. Then he took us up into the bell tower. Looking out over the broad expanse of the campus with its handsome stone buildings, he threw out his chest and said, "Look what we built—me and Mr. Duke!" Unlettered man that he was, he felt a sense of real significance in being a part of so gigantic an enterprise. It is not otherwise with you. You may feel small and insignificant yourself; but here is the biggest thing in all the world, the Church of the living Christ, and you are a part of it.

Remember, the worth of a flagpole depends not upon the wood that's in it but upon the flag that's on it. The flag that you fly tells you that you are God's child, it reminds you that your life can be redeemed for a better tomorrow, and it calls you to give yourself to something greater than yourself. If a man wants most of all to feel significant, then the psalmist has the answer.

II

So much for Mr. Adler. Here comes Mr. Freud to tell us that what we want most of all is not so much to feel significant, as to be loved. Of course the two are not unrelated. One reason why we want to be loved is, being loved by someone, we are therefore important to that person; and being loved by that person enhances our own sense of importance, and therefore satisfies our need to feel significant.

But the desire to be loved has ground to stand on that belongs to itself alone. A friend told me once how he found this out. He said that success had been his one desire; not the cheap kind of success, but the real kind of being successful in fulfilling the duty which God had placed upon him. He was so busy in that business that he had never taken time to get married. Because he had applied himself zealously to his task his work was recognized, and he was offered a promotion by his company. He was human, and of course he enjoyed the pleasure of recognition. It boosted his sense of importance. But he said that when he climbed into his car to leave the scene of his labors and drive to the place of his promotion, the pleasure of the larger position turned to dust and ashes in his hand because the seat beside him was vacant. He had achieved a sense of significance, but he still needed and wanted someone to share it with him. We want to feel significant undoubtedly, but we want to be loved too.

We are more conscious of this demand at first on the physical level, and the pity of it is that so many never rise above this level. The difference in people is not so much in what they want as in the way in which they try to get what they want, and those who try to find the answer to this fundamental need of human nature on the lower level turn love into lust and find life going sour on their hands. Physical love is only a scaffolding by means of which a more permanent structure can be built. When the

19

scaffolding comes down love lives on because it has achieved a mutuality not only of body but of spirit.

When once we see that the desire to be loved can find its answer not only in the physical, but in the spiritual as well, then the door is opened to the necessity of a real religious experience. "No longer do I call you servants," says Jesus, "but I have called you friends." Whenever you are lonely and need a friend; when your heart feels starved for want of love; then the Lord shall fulfill your desire. Someone asked a young Englishman how he knew Christ was risen and he answered, "I spent twenty minutes with him this morning." One of the aftergleams of the Resurrecction is that he still lives, and he lives to be your friend.

We all enjoy a good love story, and the greatest love story in the world is the gospel. It is the greatest because it is the story of the greatest love in the world. I heard a cynic say once that if you wanted romance that would last, you had better fall in love with yourself because that was the only kind of love that would live on. I had not the heart to remind her that she had no way of knowing because she had never married. She had just enough truth on her side to make her statement seem valid as incidents across the years gave it illustration. We are not limited to the unpredictable love of another or the unsatisfying love of self. There is the love of God you can bank on, and it will never let you down.

The hymnbook is filled with the love songs men and women have written to God—"What a Friend We Have in Jesus"; "Jesus, Lover of My Soul"; "Jesus, Thou Joy of Loving Hearts"; and others. When finally you fall in love with him yourself; when amid the uncertainties of human friends you feel the constancy of his love; then you will find yourself talking poetry in your prayers.

III

So much for Mr. Adler and Mr. Freud. Here comes Mr. Jung to tell us that what we want most is neither to feel significant nor to be loved, but to feel secure. Surely this last is basic. Any observing parent knows that no discomfort can fall upon a little one quite so distressing as the sense of physical insecurity. They tell us that a child is born with only two fears, and one is that of falling, of being let down, of being insecure. One young baby's dangerous nervousness was completely cured by following the wise counsel of a physician. He simply advised that the child be tightly wrapped in a blanket so that he could feel himself held together and protected.

The first and deepest desire of human nature is for security. We never outgrow it, and we seek in various ways to find it. This is the desire which makes it possible for you insurance men to sell so many policies. People want a feeling of security for themselves and those whom they love. One company takes the word "Security" for its name, and advertises itself as the means of taking the "if" out of "life." Anything which can take the *if* out of life and substitute for it a sense of certainty will always find a multitude of customers. The desire for security is the reason why some women marry—to achieve a sense of economic certainty. It is the reason why we are willing to pay high taxes to support a gigantic military defense—to provide national security. It is the reason some people drink liquor—to overcome a consciousness of insecurity and to achieve, even for a moment, a false stability.

The common error in all our thinking is that we find security in either things or people. We can save our money and build a bank account, but a depression or a time of inflation can wipe it out. We can bank on a friend, but disease can take him away. We can build a big army, but some other nation can build a

21

bigger one. The truth of the matter is that life is such that security on these levels will always prove futile. The earth, says the psalmist, is founded upon the seas, and established upon the floods. Foundations that are material will always prove fluid and unsubstantial. If you are going to ride out this thing called life, you need the spiritual equivalent of sea legs. Does the fact that the United States has the lead in atomic weapons, or the fact that you have a large insurance policy, make you feel secure now? Isn't there always the fear that the Russians will pull a sneak attack, or that your company will fail, or the dollar prove worthless? Are you really secure until security is an inner thing, a thing of the spirit, a certainty that though the mountains shake and the earth be removed there is nothing, absolutely nothing, which can damage or destroy the citadel of your soul?

That is not the business of the insurance company or the Department of Defense. It is the business of religion. "Therefore whosoever heareth these sayings of mine, and doeth them, I will liken him unto a wise man, which built his house upon a rock: And the rain descended, and the floods came, and the winds blew, and beat upon that house; and it fell not: for it was founded upon a rock."

During the early days of the war in the Pacific a soldier came home on leave from Guadalcanal, where the unorthodox methods of warfare and snipers behind every tree were ruining the morale of our troops. He was called to Washington and asked by the authorities if he had any suggestions as to how men could be trained to meet the demands of jungle warfare. The answer he gave brought the War Department to attention. "Yes," he said, "teach them the twenty-third psalm." "The Lord is my shepherd, I shall not want. . . . Yea, though I walk through the valley of the shadow of death, I will fear no evil: for thou art with me."

Someone to stand by! An inner companionship that gives invisible means of support! An interior resource of spiritual power that gives security!

Here are three things you want above all others: a sense of significance, the feeling of being loved, and a sense of security. These are not the things you ought to want; they are the things you do want. Your life will be determined by the ways in which you seek to find what you want. There are good ways, and there are ways that are less good. There is an old song we used to sing that went like this: when you get what you want, you don't want it. If you have found that to be true; if the wine of life has gone sour on you, and the gold has lost its glitter; then try another way, God's way. For the Lord "will fulfil the desire of them that fear him."

Is It Right for Me
to Love Myself?

"Thou shalt love they neighbour as thyself."—*Mark 12:31*

WE BEGIN WITH A QUESTION YOU HAVE ASKED MANY TIMES: IS IT right for me to love myself? The question is difficult to answer because it seems to bring into focus a conflict between two of your strongest desires.

First of all, there is your desire for your own well-being. Self-preservation is the first law of nature, and you would be dishonest if you tried to force yourself to deny that you wished the best for yourself and those whom you love. God made you, and God placed this self-regarding instinct within you, and the only honest thing to do is look it in the face and admit it is there. You were made to love yourself and you cannot help doing so.

On the other hand, alongside your desire for your own well-being, there is also your desire to stand well in the sight of God, and that fact creates a problem. It creates a problem because you have read statements in the Bible about "hating" yourself. For example, Jesus said one day: "If any man come to me, and hate not his father, and mother, and wife, and children, and brethren, and sisters, yea, and his own life also, he cannot be my disciple."

How then can you love yourself, as God made you to do, and at the same time square yourself with these words which come from the Son of God?

The answer appears to lie along the line of understanding the real meaning of what Jesus said, and then of looking at another of his very own words. When he spoke of "hating" your own life he did not mean a literal hatred but rather a lesser love; so that the person who becomes his disciple must love his Lord more than he loves himself. Then when you come to the words of our text you find a definite command to love yourself. "Thou shalt love thy neighbour as thyself." We have the habit of seeing the word "neighbour" in this verse and of overlooking the word "self." But our Lord was a wise person. He had respect for reality and he did not fail to see the regard for self with which we are born. What he is saying in the text is this: You must love yourself well, and then see to it that you love your neighbor equally as well. It is impossible to love your neighbor properly unless you love yourself well.

I

For one thing, notice that you must love yourself in order to live with your neighbor; for if you hate yourself, your mind will play a trick on you and transfer that hatred to your friends. The doctors tell us that many of our problems in human relations are caused by people who do not like themselves.

Dr. John Sutherland Bonnell, pastor of the Fifth Avenue Presbyterian Church in New York, says that after a church service a teacher came up and said to him, "I would like you to pray for me because I am terribly lonely and feel that I cannot pray to God for myself. I have no friends now in this city. Your sermon made me feel that my loneliness might be helped." He then asked her how it came about that she had no friends and she replied, "There was a time when I had friends, but I have lost them all. In the last four years they have all become estranged . . . . I haven't got a friend left in the world, I haven't even God any more."

"How do you account for the fact that you lost God and all your friends?" Dr. Bonnell asked.

"They have no use for me," she repiled, "because I have become so bitter with them. I have said and written hateful, cutting things."

"You didn't really want to hurt these friends of yours, did you?" he asked.

"No," she said. "That is the strange part of it. The last thing in the world I wanted to do was to offend or to injure them, but something in me drove me to it. Every time I said these nasty things I was sorry for it the moment they were uttered but I couldn't bring myself to tell them so. It's terribly hard for me to go back and apologize."

Dr. Bonnell says that on further questioning she admitted that she had been having trouble with her landlord, with her servant in the home, with her grocer, and others. She had fallen out with a wide variety of people. "After she had given me these facts there was a prolonged silence, and then I said to her quietly, 'Tell me now, why do you hate yourself so much?'"

She looked up with a surprised expression on her face and answered, "Who said I hated myself?"

Dr. Bonnell answered, "I know you do. Your bitterness to others is hatred of yourself that you have projected on to others and on to God."

Without lifting her head she replied: "I do hate myself but I never realized that I had projected it on to my friends and that this is the explanation of my bitterness to others."

"Do you want me to know still more about you?" he asked. When she replied that she did he said to her: "Tell me about that wretched affair you got into three or four years ago which brought all this to a head."

She admitted that there was such an affair with a married man and that she felt guilty. Dr. Bonnell spoke to her of the mercy of God in forgiveness, and as they knelt in prayer together she asked that it might be hers. Rising from her knees, she said, "I feel as though some intolerable weight that was crushing the very life out of me had been lifted from my heart. I know that things will be different in the future. I am going to write to my friend who came to this country with me and ask for her forgiveness as I have asked God's forgiveness."

Dr. Bonnell then goes on to say something which turns on a light for many of us. "Whenever one finds an individual who has become a fount of bitterness, taunting and criticizing people, saying cruel things that wound the hearts of friends, one may be sure that he is dealing with someone who hates himself, who loathes and despises himself, and that the bitterness manifested by such a person is but the projection of his own contempt for himself." [1]

In the light of that fact look again at our question, "Is it right for me to love myself?" and you see immediately that you have not only a right but a duty, because you can never love your neighbor properly until you love yourself well.

II

Move on and note, in the second place, that love to your neighbor demands that you love yourself, in order to make your largest contribution to his well-being.

Dr. Stanley Jones said that a missionary asked him this question: "Does not the gospel teach us utterly to repudiate the self, to crucify it: How then are you to love it?" Dr. Jones said his answer was simple: "These two are not contradictory. There is a lower, base, sinful self, produced through wrong acts and habits, that has to be repudiated and crucified. But this is a false, unnatural self; it is not the real self. The real self, cleansed of the incubus of this unnatural self, is to be loved and developed

---

[1] *Pastoral Psychiatry*, New York: Harper & Brothers, 1938. Used by permission.

. . . . If you did not love yourself," he went on, "you would not take care of yourself, or develop yourself, or even wash your face." And if you do not develop yourself, so that you let yourself go, refusing to take an education and declining to cultivate your capacities, then you wrong your neighbor, whether he be a member of your family or a member of the community; for unless you are your best self, your neighbor will be the loser. Jesus said: "For their sakes I sanctify myself." A true follower of his will say: "For their sakes I will make myself my best self."

At this point our text touches upon a topic on which many good Christians are mixed up. That is the subject of self-denial. We read a verse like this one: "Whosoever will come after me, let him deny himself." We take that to mean that in order to follow Christ we are called upon to deny ourselves every good thing. But then there is another verse which says: "God, who giveth us richly all things to enjoy." How can we reconcile the two? By seeing that Jesus is talking about something much more fundamental than we think. What he is asking us to give up is just ourselves. We are to deny ourselves first place and give him first place. After that, we have a duty to make whatever use of the good things of earth which will best help us to develop ourselves to the point of making our largest contribution to the worth-whileness of life around us.

I remember discussing this very problem some time ago with a friend who was considerably bothered about it. He was a real Christian if ever there was one; he had grown up with this idea which so many good Christians have, that the duty of self-denial made it wrong for him or his family to enjoy the good things of earth. The very fact that he was a good Christian and that he did his work well had brought him a large income. But did he have a right to buy the things his money could buy and give his children advantages he could well afford to give them?

Together we discussed this verse wherein our Lord tells us that we are to love ourselves well in order to love our neighbors properly. He began to see that if he had not loved himself well enough to accept the medical education which made him a good doctor, and which equipped him for the large practice he enjoyed, he would thereby have denied his professional services to the large number of patients he had been able to help. He began to think then of his children. He has a growing boy, and if that boys needs a tennis racquet with which to play in order to build a strong body, then he ought to have it. No school he sends his boy to is too good for him. If he denies his son the best education he can give him, the boy will not be able to give his best to his future life's work. He will, to that extent, rob the boy of making his largest contribution to his neighbors.

There is one sense, you see, in which you can run this business of self-denial into the ground. Long years ago I read a story about a man who took this word of Jesus about denial of self and made it the biggest thing in his life. He thought that in order to get to heaven he had to deny himself everything he really wanted. And he meant business. He actually lived up to his goal. He did deny himself everything, and one day he stood at the gateway to heaven. At last he had achieved his ambition. But as he stood there, preparing to enter, he realized that he wanted very much to get into heaven; and if he ought to deny himself everything he wanted, then he must give up this also, and turned round and walked away.

There comes a point at which self-denial is wrong and self-improvement a duty commanded by Christ. Thou shalt love thyself well enough to make the most of thyself for Christ's sake, which means to the good of your neighbor.

III

Move on now and notice a third fact: you cannot love yourself well unless you love your neighbor properly.

Up to this point we have talked about nothing but loving yourself, and there is a deep instinct which tells you that Christ did not come to tell us to center ourselves upon ourselves. Your good sense tells you that there is a great deal more to Christianity than loving ourselves, and of course there is.

The beauty about the teaching of Jesus is that it is so well-balanced. He knows that each of us is a field on which two sets of instincts are at play. There are the egoistic instincts, suggested by the word "ego," meaning "I," and which force us to have regard for ourselves. There are also the altruistic instincts, suggested by the word, "alter," meaning "others," and which force us to have regard for others. Our job is somehow to find a balance between the two. To try to live entirely for others is to be unhappy; for those who try to do so find their own selves intruding, and it makes them miserable. To try to live entirely for yourself is to be unhappy also, because it denies and fails to develop that part of your being which is altrustic. Jesus says, "Thou shalt love thy neighbour as thyself." Love yourself well, and then love your neighbor equally as well. While there are some of us who need to be told to love ourselves, there are others who need to be told it is wrong not to love our neighbor.

Fannie Hurst, the writer, says that "one evening at dinner, after my husband had related a decision he had made during the day, I burst forth with: 'How is it that in all the years I never remember you doing a thing I wish you hadn't done? How can you be so consistently mindful of others?' 'I suppose it's because I have to live with myself,' he replied."

You and I will begin to see the sense in what Jesus says when we understand the reason it is wrong not to love our neighbor. If we love ourselves so that we center ourselves upon ourselves with no thought of our neighbor, we develop into a self we cannot live with. I think the most miserable person I know is a man who is all wrapped up in himself. He reminds me of the old legend concerning a father who left home on a long trip and whose going-away present to his son was a picture of the boy himself. When the father returned, the boy had starved to death because he was so much absorbed in his own picture. You know people like that.

On the other hand, the happiest people you know are those who love their neighbor as they love themselves. They have balanced that concern for themselves with a corresponding concern for other folks. They live in a house where there are windows as well as mirrors. I heard a man who admittedly lived pretty much for himself, say after he had gone out of his way to do a kindness for his friends: "It made me feel so good inside I wondered why I didn't do the same kind of thing every day." On TV we are advised each week to buy various cure-alls and feel good again. More of us would get the same result with a little of this medicine the Great Physician has for us in our text.

Luke tells of a lawyer asking Jesus what he must do to inherit eternal life. Jesus answered something like this: Love God with everything that's in you, and your neighbor as yourself. The man wanted to know then, Who is my neighbor? In answer Jesus drew him the picture of the good Samaritan, who found a fellow in need, and who went out of his way to do something for him.

31

There are plenty of people in need all around you every day: in need of a kind word, of the warmth of your friendship, of a cup of cold water for the heat of the journey. Before you let this day go by, pass a resolution that you will not pass by on the other side—that you will stop long enough to answer his need.

Love yourself well, and your neighbor equally well, and you will find that deep contentment which comes from knowing you have done the will of God, and so fulfilled the needs of your own nature.

How Can I Learn
to Take It?

"We triumph even in our troubles."—*Rom. 5:3* (Moffatt)

FROM SOMEWHERE OUT OF THE PAST COMES THE STORY OF A GREAT sultan who had his grand scribe compile a history of the human race. With long toil the task was accomplished, and the scribe went to the sultan with one hundred donkeys laden with five hundred volumes of historic lore. When the sultan saw such a mountainous mass of material he was displeased and wanted his history cut down to readable proportions. "Abridge! Abridge!" commanded the angry potentate. "Sire," answered the historian, "all these volumes may be compressed into a single sentence: 'They were born; they suffered; they died.'"

Without pressing to exaggerated conclusions this summary of existence, everyone knows the truth of the historian's comment. It is not true because Job said it, but Job said it because it is true: "Man is born unto trouble, as the sparks fly upward." Every son of Adam meets with enough pain and misfortune and mental anguish to assure him that life is not a bottle of perfume by a long sea mile. The school of experience has its own colors, and they are black and blue. As soon as you matriculate in the university of life you discover that one of the required courses is called trouble.

In view of that fact, the part of wisdom is not to play the ostrich and refuse to see the fact; it is rather to accept it and see what can be done about it. Of all the lessons that must be learned, the one which means most to our personal well-being is this: how to deal with unwelcome experiences which are part of the facts of life. So we go back to our Christian faith to learn what it says about being able to take it.

33

I

Many people who are having trouble with life begin by putting their problem in the form of the question, Why? Here, for example, is a letter that one man wrote to a friend of mine. He said that he was seventy-four years of age and he listed five catastrophes which had befallen members of his family, and then he closed with this: "My question about life can be summed up in this one word: Why?"

That is the approach which most of us make toward misfortune, and it is not difficult to understand the reason. We started out with the idea that religion explains everything. We were taught to think of it first of all as a set of theoretical propositions intended to clear up the mystery of life, to make it possible to answer all ultimate problems, and to enable us to say, "I now understand why." When we were children and could be content with simple answers, religion was presented as the answer to our question, Why? Why was there ever anything at all? Why did God make the world? Why are we here? Why do we suffer? Why die? For every question that was raised, religious faith was given as the answer and the idea sank in: religion is a way of explaining everything.

Now, however, the years have passed and every year the mystery of life grows more profound. We have seen such tragedy as we never dreamed existed when we were younger. We constantly happen upon the rankest injustice: innocent lives blasted into bits and high hopes dashed into the dust; persons whom we think deserve from fate a hand with kings and queens having continually to take all the low cards in the deck. In the innocent years of childhood, God was in his heaven and all was right with the world; but now it has become plain that life is far from being a musical comedy. There are times when the whole business seems out of joint and Christian faith fails to answer our questions.

During the summer of 1929, while serving as student assistant in a church, I visited a hospital one day and found in the corridor a mother whose child was ill. Inside the room he lay on his bed, tortured with pain. She was an intelligent Christian and a Sunday-school teacher, and had always thought of her faith as something that would answer all of her questions. But now bewilderment was written large in her face. Why should her innocent child be forced to suffer so? She had gone to her Bible, and she had prayed, and she had read books about God; still she was in the dark. Because her faith had failed to clear up the mystery, she was almost at the point of throwing it overboard altogether.

Let me say that I have the fullest sympathy with everyone who is living in the land of Why. I have been a resident there myself and I know the agony of it. I know that you are dealing here with one of the ultimate problems of human thought. It is called the problem of suffering and it is stated like this: Why, if God is good and powerful, does he permit good people to suffer and bad people to prosper? It is called an ultimate problem because no one, from Job on down, has ever been able to find a full answer. I know too that while resentment against providence is natural, as long as you make no other approach to your trouble you will remain at a standstill. You will get nowhere. You will have to learn to adopt a method which is at once more intelligent and more courageous and more Christian.

II

What is that method? It is to see that you are following the wrong cue in putting your problem in the form of the question, Why? It is to see that the Christian faith nowhere promises to clear up all mysteries. It is to accept the fact, as Paul puts it, that "at present we only see the baffling reflections in a mirror"; and it is to remember that our Lord himself was faced with the same question. There are times with some of us that the most comforting passage in the whole of the Bible is the cry of Jesus from the cross: "My God, my God why, . . . ?" He never said, "I have explained the universe." What he said was in effect, "I have overcome it, risen above it, won a spiritual victory in the face of it." If you are a Christian in the sense that you will let him call the signals you will see that the big question is no longer Why?, but How? It is not "why" do I have to be on the receiving end of so much trouble; but "how" can I face it so as to rise above it? The method, in brief, is to move out of the land of Why into the country of How.

For example, see how one man changed his Why to How. In our times there can have been few men who knew more trouble than Cardinal Desiré Joseph Mercier, of Belgium. Of all his difficult days, none could have been harder than that one in Rome when the news reached him of the destruction of his own city: the nave of his cathedral a mass of ruins, his home torn by shells, the priceless books of his library burned, and the bodies of his peaceful students cremated. Cardinal Mercier was not one to take things lying down. He had in him tremendous capacities for resentment and indignation, and those who were with him in the first few minutes of his misery say that the complaints rose deep out of his wretchedness. "Why all this sorrow, O Lord? My God, my God, why hast thou forsaken us?" Then, they say, his eye fell on the crucifix, and the stormy man grew still. It was as though once again the Christ had calmed the tempest, and they heard him say: "The disciple is not above his master, nor the servant above his Lord. We will rebuild." He had moved out of the land of Why into the country of How.

III

When you come to the point you are ready to make this move you can remember this fact: it is possible to transfer the center of your life into an area where you are not at the mercy of what the world can do to you. In wide realms of experience the world has the upper hand. It can blind you, burn you, and mash you under its heel. But there is an inner area where you are not at the mercy of the world. There, though the world is still great and strong, you are greater and stronger. Lawrence the Martyr, for example, was roasted to death on a gird. After they had had him over a slow fire for some time, so the story runs, he looked up at his torturers and said whimsically, "Turn me over. That side is done." He had succeeded in moving the center of his life into an area where he was not at the mercy of his torturers. Now the secret of such a victory lies in the insight that the big thing in life is not what happens to you, but in the way you take what happens to you. The New Testament has two truths which will help you to put this to work.

The first is in the statement of our text. Paul says this: "We triumph even in our troubles, knowing that trouble produces endurance, endurance produces character." (Moffatt)

What that means is this: if you set yourself primarily to seek character, and to grow a soul, you can use any experience short of death and insanity that the world can present you. Out of any situation you can emerge a better person, if that is what you want. If you are primarily after wealth, the world can whip you. If you are primarily after pleasure, the world can defeat you. If you are primarily after fame, the world can banish you to your St. Helena. But if you are primarily growing a soul, you

37

can then capitalize on anything life does to you. Happiness can make you more radiant; bereavement can leave you more wise, more sympathetic, more understanding. All things can be made to work together for good, for your real good; and so you, like Paul, triumph in trouble, knowing that trouble produces endurance, and endurance produces character.

Dr. Stanley Jones says he watched an eagle in the Himalaya Mountains one day when a storm struck. He expected the eagle to be dashed to death against the rocks by the fury of the wind, but instead, the eagle set his wings in such a way that the harder the wind blew the higher he rose by it.

The ability to capitalize on adverse winds when the storms begin to blow is one of the secrets of our faith. The sacred writer tells us that our Lord himself was made perfect through suffering. If you will remember that according to Jesus the purpose of life is not comfort but character, you can head toward that and make anything serve your aim. You can be like the man who one day met a wolf at the door and came out wearing a fur coat.

Most often we try to run in the wrong gear. We say to ourselves: We are whipped, beaten, up against it, circumstances are too strong for us. We try to serve God, and all we get for it is a peck of trouble. Paul might have said that but he didn't. What he did was shift gears from low to high. He said something like this, "Life is intended to make a man of me, and any situation can be used for that end." On that gear you can make the grade and find yourself on top of the world; you will know that even if the worst happens, it can be turned into the best.

Walk through a second door and you will discover that the New Testament has a further truth. The time came when Paul found himself in prison in Rome. He had always wanted to go to Rome to proclaim his good news in the metropolis of the world, but he had not planned to go there as a jailbird. Yet it is hard to keep a good man down, and before you knew it this little crippled Christian was making his influence felt among members of the prison guard. When he wrote his Letter to his friends in Philippi you find him saying: "I want you to know, brethren, that what has happened to me has really served to advance the gospel, so that it has become known throughout the whole praetorian guard and to all the rest that my imprisonment is for Christ; and most of the brethren have been made confident in the Lord because of my imprisonment, and are much more bold to speak the word of God without fear." (R.S.V.)

What the apostle is saying is this: not only is it possible to use your tough breaks so that they make a better man of you, but you can also use them so that they become an opportunity to do something for other people. "Most of the brethren have become confident in the Lord because of my imprisonment." If, when you find yourself imprisoned within the confines of some hated handicap or cruel providence, you remember what Helen Keller has meant to blind people, and you begin to ask yourself: how can I handle this thing so as to keep others like myself from losing their faith but rather make them confident in the Lord; then you will see your imprisonment not as something to be despised but as an opportunity for a much needed service. The very challenge of it will speak to the hero in your soul and give you courage.

In 1937 when I went to Northfield, Massachusetts, people were still talking about the tragedy which had occurred three years before. Elliott Speer, headmaster of Mt. Hermon School, had been shot and killed one night by an unknown person, and the mysterious murder has never yet been solved.

Elliott Speer was the son of Dr. Robert E. Speer, the apostle of world missions in the Northern Presbyterian Church. His biographer writes that the greatest test of his Christian faith and character was the tragic death of his son. Concerning it, he wrote to a friend: "One's only and adequate light is to think of what God allowed to happen in the life of His Own dear Son and to be sure that even out of the deepest evil He can bring good."

Several years later, during the war, Dr. Speer was speaking at Montreat one Sunday morning. His text was the psalmist's question: "If the foundations be destroyed what can the righteous do?" In the congregation I saw parents whose sons had been lost in the war, and I'm sure they were thinking that the foundations had been destroyed and their faith was being tested severely. Dr. Speer made no reference to his own tragedy; but everybody there was thinking about it, and he knew it. I shall never forget one answer he gave to the psalmist's question. "When the foundations are destroyed, what can the righteous do?" "Well," he said, "they can go on being righteous." They can hold on to their faith in the love of God, and go on being strong. That is what Dr. Speer was doing, and by so doing he helped other fathers and mothers remain confident in the Lord. He could not explain such a tragedy but he was able to overcome it; and by overcoming it, he turned it into an opportunity to prove to other men and women the livableness of life.

There are times when you cannot keep from asking Why to save your life. That is natural, and you need not blame yourself for doing this; you are entitled to all the light you can get. But you will be a much happier person if you make up your mind to move out of the land of Why into the country of How. When you do, you will find that Paul is a good man to get to know.

How Can I Find
Strength for the Day?

"As thy days, so shall thy strength be."—*Deut. 33:25*

DURING THE PAST TEN YEARS LETTERS IN RESPONSE TO RADIO BROAD-
casts have come to my desk from many parts of the country.
These letters indicate that one of the problems many people face
constantly is how to find strength for the day. That is the question to which we will address ourselves in this chapter.

Fortunately, there is one fact that we have to fall back upon,
and that is that very few people ordinarily live up to the limit
of their resources. Students of human nature like William James
have been telling us for years that we are capable of far more
strength than we usually make use of; that there is a reserve, a
potential, a backlog of energy we are not accustomed to check
on, and that had we the wisdom and the will to do so, we might
surprise even ourselves in our ability to do or to endure.

Such a fact seems the best angle from which to approach our
present problem. We find encouragement in the Bible where
God speaks to his people and gives them this promise: "As thy
days, so shall thy strength be." God's people are facing a difficult
task. They have been brought to the edge of the Promised Land
and now they must go in and conquer Canaan. God sends them
on with these words sounding in their ears: "As thy days, so
shall thy strength be." There were times no doubt when those
words made the difference between quitting and keeping on. We
can consider several ways in which they might do the same to us.

I

For one thing, they tell us that God promises power for each
day's needs. The emphasis is on the *now*. "As thy days [mean-
ing, as thy todays], so shall thy strength be." As long as we limit

ourselves to the needs of the present, we can find power to get through.

Few of us have the wisdom to do that. We place a double load on our minds and seek to carry not only the burdens of the present but those of the past. One popular way by which the past projects itself into the present and adds its weight to the burdens of today is the matter of reviewing and regretting old decisions. Many of our most important decisions have to be made without the benefit of experience to guide us, decisions like the choice of a lifework and of the person we marry. We have never passed that way before, and we enter, as it were, an uncharted country.

If the road we are following becomes steep or indistinct, we instantly raise the question whether it is the right road. Suppose we had chosen the other career or married the other person, or settled in one town instead of another? We bring up these questions out of the past and wear ourselves out reviewing and regretting them.

There are two ways by which we can handle these specters from the past. One is to remind ourselves that we know nothing of the road not taken. We imagine it is a fine, straight road, and that if we had followed it we should have arrived at the land of heart's desire. But that is pure supposition. The road not taken might have been longer and more wearisome than the road you did choose. Had we taken the other road twenty years ago every subsequent choice in our lives would have been different, and there is just as much reason for saying that life, as a whole, would have proved less satisfying as there is for saying that it would have proved more satisfying. We have all met the golfer who says, "If my drive had been straight, I would have made that hole in par." But the man forgets that if his drive had been different every other shot would have been different too. We know nothing of the road not taken.

Neither do we know anything of the future of the road we are following. We are supposing it is always hard and steep, but who can tell whether we shall not turn a corner tomorrow, next week, or next month, and run head-on into the happiness we thought belonged only to the other road. The text does not say, "As thy yesterdays, so shall thy strength be." It says, "As thy days . . . ."

Neither does it say, "As thy tomorrows." For every person who overloads his mind by regretting the past, there are a dozen who carry a double burden by being anxious about the future. They send their thoughts out into the unknown, and because it is unknown, they begin to imagine the worst. Will my health hold out? Will my job fold up? Can I possibly measure up to the task and the responsibilities which I face? What does it mean when for three weeks I haven't heard a word from my boy away from home?

Just as Paul tells us to forget the things that are behind and cease regretting the past, so does Jesus counsel to take no anxious thought for the morrow and cease worrying about the future. It does no good, you know—"Which of you by taking thought can add one cubit unto his stature?"—and tomorrow will have trouble enough of its own—"Sufficient unto the day is the evil thereof."

The text does not say, "As thy yesterdays," nor, "As thy tomorrows." It says, "As thy days, so shall thy strength be." When we learn to limit the load on our minds by unloading the past and future and concentrating upon the present, we shall find, according to the promise, that there is strength sufficient for each day's need.

II

In the second place, we can tap the resources of our text by remembering that we have to face only one task at a time. Granted that even though we have got the past and the future off our hands, there is still the present, and the demands of the present are terrifying. Even so, no matter how busy life may be, we will never have to face more than one task at a time. Moments always approach us in single file, never in a crowd. In a given instant of time only one demand can possibly deserve attention.

Here is a fact which often we overlook when we are tired and apprehensive and overburdened. We find ourselves saying in a mood of defeatism: "How can I ever get through this impossible day? Look at the myriad of things I must do before night. A dozen business problems, a score of letters to write, and all day long an unbroken line of people trying to sell me something I do not want to buy. A life like this is too much for human endurance."

Whenever I am tempted to that sort of bottleneck, I always recall an old Chinese proverb which says, "One at a time is good fishing"; also that other word out of the past, "The longest journey begins with a single step." Dr. Norman Vincent Peale says that at his summer home the garage is two hundred yards from the house and at night it is pitch dark when the lights of the car are turned off and the garage doors are shut. "I carry a flashlight," he says, "to find my way. I have discovered that the most effective way to use my flashlight is to throw its illumination upon the path immediately in front of me. If I lift it and throw it far ahead, its beam is soon dissipated in the darkness and I find myself stumbling. When I am content to light up merely the next step or two, I keep on the path and come quickly and safely to the house." Taking a step at a time, whether on a dark path or a busy schedule, is the best means of progress.

Look now at that terrifyingly heavy day through the eyes of this simple truth. Any man can dictate one letter at a time, resolutely refusing to think of the second until the first is finished. Any man can make one decision at a time, refusing to consider the second until the first is out of the way. Any man can see one solicitor at a time, refusing to give thought to the others until the first is dealt with. Any woman can plan one meal at a time, refusing to think of dinner until lunch is out of the way. One of the busiest men I know, and a man who accomplishes a tremendous amount of labor—writing books, preparing sermons, delivering lectures—tells me this is his secret. He plans his day's work, listing each task separately, always the most difficult at the beginning, and then goes down the list one at a time.

Archer Wallace says that at the request of friends in California he went to see an old lady in a home for incurables in a Canadian city. He found her in a rather bare room and suggested that they go out on the veranda while he told her of her old friends. "I have never been out on the veranda," she said; "I have a spinal condition which prevents my being moved." This seemed a cruel condition to Mr. Wallace, and he asked her how long she had been there. "Twenty-six years," she answered. He thought of twenty-six years and of all that had happened in his life in so long a time.

"Do you mean to tell me that you have never been out of this small room in twenty-six years?"

"I have never been over the threshold since I was brought here twenty-six years ago."

"There are times," writes Mr. Wallace, "when conversation seems out of place and this was one of them. It seemed anything

I might say would sound formal and insincere. Then that woman said something I shall never want to forget.

"She said, 'It only comes one day at a time and God is so good.' Twenty-six years of almost continual suffering, and yet she found strength for the days, because she met them one at a time."

Says the poet,

> God broke the years to hours and days,
> That hour by hour
> And day by day,
> Just going on a little way,
> We might be able all along
> To keep quite strong.[1]

"As thy days, so shall thy strength be."

III

Go on, in the third place, and note that there is still something to be said. Strength for the day comes by sloughing off the past and future and limiting the load on the mind to the present. It also comes by facing the demands of the present one at a time. But suppose one of these single-file duties proves more difficult than we had anticipated. Then we can fall back on the fact that new situations create by calling forth new powers. When we do our best in giving the strength we have, we can always count on God to supply the rest.

Almost any mother can verify this truth. She spends her energy caring for her children, and then one night she goes to bed so tired she says she could not lift another finger if her life depended upon it. But during the night one of the children gets sick, desperately sick, so that for days and nights, and for weeks

---

[1] George Klingle, "Hour by Hour," from *Best Loved Religious Poems.*

on end, she has to nurse him, and all the while the only rest she gets is in snatches. But she does it. She finds that new situations create new powers by calling them forth, and that when we do our best God supplies the rest.

The human body is endowed with certain glands which, when a physical emergency arises, secrete and supply an added element which enables us to meet the emergency. So Professor Mc-Dougall tells about a boy who, chased across a field by an infuriated bull, succeeded in leaping a high fence and saving himself. Some time later the boy returned to that locality and, finding the fence still standing, he attempted to jump it without the stimulus of danger. He couldn't do it; the reason he was able to before was because his glands came to his rescue.

The same thing seems to be true on higher levels. The same God who puts the endocrine glands in the body puts something like them in the spirit, so that when a new need arises a new power is given. That is what a preacher in New York means when he delivers a sermon to his people on the subject, "You Are Braver Than You Think." That is what the wisdom of the human race means when it says that "Man's extremity is God's opportunity." That is what the psalmist means when he says, "Thou preparest a table before me in the presence of mine enemies." That is what Mr. Moody meant when someone asked him if he had dying grace. "No," he answered, "now I have living grace, but when I come to die I shall be given dying grace." That is what God meant when he said to Paul, in answer to the request that his thorn in the flesh be taken away: "No, I'll not take it away but I'll do something else: I'll give you strength to bear it. My *grace* is sufficient for you." That is what a member of a church I once served meant in a conversation we had while I was visiting in her home. She was still in middle life but even at that I had buried her husband several years before. It was a happy marriage which was thus cut off midway. She has one son, an only child, and when I was talking with her she told me she hadn't seen him since he went away to the army six months before. This is what she said: "You know, you think you can't stand these things, but when they come, you can." And she smiled when she said it.

Here, then, is your promise of strength for the day. It is his promise, and it will not fail. It says that somewhere back behind life, and over and above and beneath life, is God. He is not far away, but just close by, and he says, Take these words and go and live on them: "As thy days, so shall thy strength be"—for underneath are the everlasting arms.

How Can I Deal
with Grief?

"In the world ye shall have tribulation: but be of good cheer; I have overcome the world."—*John 16:33*

SEVERAL YEARS AGO A GROUP OF DOCTORS KNOWN AS NEUROPSYCHIA-trists met for their annual session. It was my pleasure to be present and one of the papers read was entitled "Grief Reaction." It interested me to know that these doctors were concerned with what happens to a member of the family when the shock of bereavement strikes, and I felt that here was a theme to which a minister might well give thought. So our topic has to do with the problem of grief.

It is a somber subject of course. There is a line in Tennyson's "In Memoriam,"

> Never morning wore
> To evening, but some heart did break

and who knows when you may be forced to face the burden of sudden bereavement? Moreover, it is possible that there are those who do not see the beauty of this day because past grief shuts out the sunshine. In looking for light upon our darkness we go back to a text from our Lord: "In the world ye shall have tribulation: but be of good cheer; I have overcome the world."

I

Christ wants us to learn to accept grief as one of the facts of life. There is a false way of looking at things which would have us believe that life is all sweetness and light, and that any trouble which intrudes upon our happiness is not real and has no place in the scheme of things. But our Lord could not be hoodwinked

49

by any such juggling of the truth. He looked the facts in the face and he saw that in the kind of world in which we live trouble is bound to come. He said it as plainly as words can make it: "In the world we shall have tribulation"—period. There is no way you can shuffle the cards and deal it out. It is there, and it is there to stay; and the part of wisdom is to see it, and to accept it, and to make up your mind calmly that grief is bound to come.

I wonder if you saw that amusing touch one of the writers reporting the Walker Cup Golf Matches in Scotland gave his article? He said that the American players would face not only the hazards of the Old Course at St. Andrews, but also cold and probable rain and a lazy wind. He went on to describe a lazy wind as one that was too lazy to go around and so it went right through you. It is not otherwise with the trouble that causes grief; it may go around you for a time, but sooner or later it will go right through you. In the world, whether you wish it or not, "ye shall have tribulation."

I went once to visit a friend whom I had known in college. In the meantime he had married and established his home where there were two children. He told me that several years before he and his wife had lost a child, just two years old. At first he was bitter and said over and over to himself, "Why did it have to happen to me and not to someone else?" Later on, he realized that there was no good reason why he should expect to be exempt, and that he then said to himself: "Why shouldn't it happen to me?" Then he found not only the deep peace which comes from acceptance, but the strength of the presence of God, which his bitterness had formerly canceled.

So then in dealing with the problem of grief, the first step is to learn to accept it as something that is bound to come.

II

The second step lies in seeking to understand the nature of the experience.

Our doctor friends can help us by pointing out reactions which are altogether normal, and so make us willing to be patient with the slow healing process of time. I remember once having a conference with a wife who had lost her husband. She told me she had accepted the loss, but that her problem lay in having no interest in life. Later on I discovered that disinterestedness in life is altogether normal and to be expected. It made me wish I had known that fact at the time, for it would have helped her. As one expert puts it: "We should anticipate *these* stages in our emotional convalescence: unbearable pain, poignant grief, empty days, resistance to consolation, disinterestedness in life, gradually giving way under the healing sunlight of love, friendship, and social challenge, to a pattern of action and the acceptance of the irresistible challenge of life."

Another characteristic of grief so common as to be mentioned by the doctors, is that often grief is accompanied by intense feelings of guilt. The sorrowing person blames himself for not giving the deceased proper care during a period of illness, for failure in some obligation, or for being responsible in some way for the cause of death. You would know how real is the anguish, if you had ever been with such a person at such a time, and had seen the look of agony on his face, and heard him say, "If only I had done this or that, it might not have happened." The reminder that you were never consciously negligent and that you always did the best you knew, plus the remembrance that a sense of guilt is often a characteristic of grief, will help lessen the load.

Oftentimes I have found another form of the sense of guilt. We are so wedded to the Old Testament idea that adversity is necessarily a sign of sin that we suppose our sorrow is God's punishment for some evil of ours. At that point it is well to remind yourself of this fact, that while all sin brings suffering, all suffering is not necessarily due to sin. The proof of that truth lies in the picture of Christ: he was sinless, but he was not without suffering. You will divide your grief in half if you can succeed in separating from it any sense of guilt.

The doctors also tell us it is important that grief be allowed to express itself. It is an emotion, and if it is bottled up and not allowed to come out it will cause a nervous restiveness and do physical damage. Rabbi Liebman puts it like this: "When we face the loss of a dear one, we should allow our hearts full leeway in the expression of their pain . . . . After all, we were given tear ducts to use for just such hours of darkness."

III

"In the world," said Jesus, "ye shall have tribulation." In the light of that fact, we would first of all accept, and then try to understand the nature of the experience. Our Lord does not stop there, however; he goes on to say this other thing: "But be of good cheer; I have overcome the world." Having made allowance for the minus that is in life, he suggests that there is a plus, and he would have us accentuate the positive. When the first shock of grief is past, it is right to begin to think about the plus.

We should remember that whatever we lose, we can be grateful for what we have already had. I heard the late Dr. Albert W. Beaven of Rochester say what this truth meant to him. He said that his seven-year-old little girl died and he and Mrs. Beaven seemed altogether unable to overcome their grief. There were so many things around the house which reminded them of her— her room, her playthings, the vacant chair at the table; and whenever they saw these things they were reminded of their loss. He said their grief was leading them further and further into gloom, and he realized that something would have to be done to preserve their health. Somehow he got hold of our truth and he said to his wife: "Instead of thinking of what we have lost, let's begin to think of what we have possessed. We have had seven years of joy from this little girl's life, and nothing that has happened can take that away from us." And so from then on the things that reminded them of their little one were made to speak of what they had possessed instead of what they had lost. On that ladder they climbed out of grief into gladness.

IV

There is a further fact which makes all the difference in the world for the Christian. Remember that if you have lost one whom you love, he is not lost. If this is really God's world, then we are under his care whether we live or whether we die. Much as we miss those we love, we can rejoice that they have found their true home in the love of God. As Marcus Aurelius put it: "It is pleasant to die, if there be gods; and sad to live, if there is none."

Here is a man named Walter Lowen who lost his wife and who wrote something of his experience for us in the *Reader's Digest*. He says:

Let me tell you what the doctor who attended my wife did for me as I stood dazed and lost at the foot of her bed, knowing not only that the 37 years we had had together were over, but feeling also that all meaning had gone from life forever. He took my arm and held it for a moment. And then he said in a matter-of-fact voice: "You'll see her again." That was all.

But it was all I needed to hear. That simple gesture and eloquent statement reminded me of the one thing that has been given to us to

53

help us bear such separations from our beloved: the resurgent and ever-present ability to believe in immortality.

The idea of immortality is the strongest lifeline to the grief-stricken. In my case I could, from his words on, think of the separation of Selma and myself as temporary. Everything that sustained that belief sustained me. Three of my friends somehow knew the almost morbid sensitivity that one in grief has; they sent flowering plants instead of cut flowers, so that the idea of continuance of life and not its brief blooming would be suggested.[1]

As our Lord put it in the long ago: "I go to prepare a place for you. And if I go and prepare a place for you, I will come again and receive you unto myself; that where I am, there ye may be also." What life is like in that land that is fairer than day we do not know, but we do not need to know; we know only that he is there, and that is enough. When a sharp pain struck the heart of Peter Marshall and he was being carried out into the night on a stretcher, he looked up into the face of his wife Catherine and said, "See you in the morning, Darling." It is the Christian's faith that though the night be dark and long, the morning will surely come, and with it a blessed reunion.

V

There is a fifth and final thing to be said. The belief in immortality is sound, and we have a right to strengthen ourselves in its assurance. Yet it is unnatural and unchristian and unhealthy to fold our hands and sit still and spend our time gazing into heaven. When our Lord stood with his men on the Mount of Olives and was taken up out of their sight, they went back to their job of carrying on for him. They did their best to do what he would have done had he remained with them. They were consciously loyal to the One they had lost and sought to continue

[1] Walter Lowen, "Please Omit Sympathy," *Reader's Digest*, March, 1955.

his life vicariously in their own work. As they did so, they were saved from the dangers of self-pity and they found the genuine satisfaction of helping to make life better for other people. Here is something, I think, for the rest of us: we can become, as Rabbi Liebman puts it, "ambassadors of our departed, their messengers and their spokesmen, carrying out the mission for which they lived and strove, and which they bequeathed to us."

The late Rufus Jones had only one son, Lowell, who died at the age of eleven, but the boy continued for forty-five years to be a dominant influence in that great man's life. Jones's study at Haverford included many photographs of the learned and famous, but the central place, over the mantel, was always occupied by the portrait of this boy. Rufus Jones felt that he had to live for both himself and his boy, and in this be succeeded to a remarkable degree. Writing more than forty years after the occasion of his sorrow, Rufus Jones told of the boy as follows: "I overheard him once talking to a group of playmates, when each one was telling what he wanted to be when grown up, and Lowell said when his turn came, 'I want to grow up and be a man like my daddy.' Few things in my life have ever touched me as those words did, or have given me a greater impulse to dedication."

Here then is the problem of grief as seen in the light of our Christian faith. You can accept it as one of the facts of life and do your best to understand it. You can remind yourself of what you have possessed, instead of thinking only of what you have lost. You can rest in the Christian's assurance of life after death and look forward to the morning of reunion. Then you can go back to your task as an ambassador of the departed. There is hardly anyone as far along as middle life who does not have one he loves there in the unseen. It may be a wife or a husband, or a mother or a father, or even a child, as it was with Rufus Jones. In the sacred silence of this moment you recall all the loveliness of that life and you know the things he would be doing were he here today in the flesh. There then is the final answer to your problem. You can substitute for him. You can step into his shoes and take his place and carry on for him. And as you do, the darkness will become light and the night will brighten into morning and you can say with our Lord, "I have overcome the world."

How Can I Get Rid
of Resentment?

"But I say to you that hear, Love your enemies, do good to those who hate you, bless those who curse you, pray for those who abuse you."—*Luke 6:27-28* (*R.S.V.*)

SEVEN YEARS AGO ONE OF THE MAJOR RADIO NETWORKS REQUESTED our church to record a thirty-minute worship service to be used on one of their regular Sunday morning broadcasts. Our choir consented to help, and a member of our church who is a radio man came down to direct us. The theme of the sermon was Abundant Life, and in the course of its development the point was made that resentment is one thief which robs people of this life to the full.

One letter which came in response raised this question: "You tell us that resentment is a thief, but you say nothing about getting rid of this robber. What we need to know is how to go about doing the thing we need to do." We want to look now at the steps which can lead us out of our resentments.

I

We go back to our Lord for guidance and we find him saying in the text that we are to love our enemies. But that is just our trouble: how can we love somebody whom we hate and against whom we are holding resentment? When we read between the lines there are two things at least which throw light on that thorny question.

The first is something which cannot be said too often. In the New Testament there are two words for "love" which carry two distinct ideas, but in the English versions they are translated exactly alike. The first of these words, "philia," puts the emphasis on the emotional aspect of love; while the second, "agape," emphasizes the volitional aspect, the determination to seek the good of the one who is loved. In the first we love a person because we like him, and in the second we love him in spite of the fact that we may not like him. That is, we entertain good will toward him and desire his welfare. Whenever in the Bible love is commanded as a duty toward our neighbor or toward our enemy, it is always this second word that is used and never the first. We can put it down as a fact that Jesus never says that we must like our neighbors or that we must have affection for our enemies. What he does is to command us to *love* our enemies—to desire their welfare, to seek their highest good—whether we like them or not. When you look at the matter in this way, it begins to throw some light on our problem. You can love your enemies in spite of the fact that you do not like them because you can control your will where you cannot command your feelings.

The second consideration which encourages you to love someone you may not like is the hardheaded, realistic fact that it is for your own good to do so. Our Lord also said: "Every one who is angry with his brother shall be in danger of the judgment." (A.S.V.) That sounds like a religious reason against anger and resentment; but when you shorten the sentence you get the real point: "Everyone who is angry with his brother shall be in danger"—period.

When a preacher says something like that you put it down as mere preaching, but when a doctor says the same thing you are more likely to listen. Listen to Dr. William Sadler: "There is simply no way to get comfort and delight out of hate—it is truly the arch-demon of all the little devils who are subversive of joy and destructive of character." Listen to Dr. John Hunter, a famous English physician, who suffered from a bad heart: "I'm at the mercy of any scoundrel who will make me angry." He was right. He got up at a medical meeting to refute something he did not like, and in a fit of anger, fell dead. Listen to Dr. Karl Menninger: "I can say from clinical experience that in some women the degree of discomfort in pregnancy . . . has been directly proportional to the intensity of their resentment to having to live through this phase of their role." Listen again to an optometrist who said to E. Stanley Jones: "Anger narrows the field of vision and shuts off the peripheral vision, so it is dangerous to drive when angry, for you can't see things that are not in the direct line of a narrowed vision." So he says that when he is angry, he pulls his car alongside the road and stays there until his anger dies down.

A man who knew how dangerous it was for him to get angry was overheard by his secretary saying to a visitor in his office: "Quick, get the mischief out of here, I can't afford to get mad at you." "Every one who is angry with his brother is in danger." The reason Jesus said that is that life says it. You just cannot get away from it. If you give a person a piece of your mind, you only lose your own peace of mind; and if you hold hate within your heart, you hold hell within it. Harry Emerson Fosdick told about a woman who went to pieces because of her resentment against her sister, and concluded: "Hating someone is like burning down your house to get rid of a rat."

So then when Jesus tells us to love our enemies we can find practical encouragement in these two facts: we need not like them in order to desire their welfare, and it is definitely to our advantage to rid ourselves of enmity.

II

The second thing he tells us is to pray for them. He adds emphasis to this second step by naming it twice. "Bless those who curse you," he says, "pray for those who abuse you." And what

Jesus preached, he practiced. It is written that on the cross he prayed for his enemies.

The word "bless" means to invoke a blessing upon. It is a prayer that God will make that person's life a blessed one. It would take someone like our Lord to think of such a thing because our human nature is so far from it. When one man wrongs another, the usual thing is not to ask that God will bless him; the far more customary thing is to link the word "God" with the word "damn," and it becomes a prayer that God will damn him. Here is a woman who told how she got rid of her resentments. Every time she thought of the person who had done her wrong, she then and there said inwardly: "I bless you—in His name." That habit is in line with the word of our Lord: "Bless those who curse you."

And then: "Pray for those who abuse you." Just exactly why our Lord added this phrase I have not been able to determine. A study of the Greek was not very helpful at this point. The only thing it said was that this word "pray" referred not so much to the content of the prayer as to its end and aim. My own guess is that Jesus named this step twice in order to emphasize its importance and then to say this: when you bring yourself to the point that you can invoke the blessing of God upon the person who has made himself your enemy, then pray for him. That is, keep on persevering in your prayer on his behalf to achieve the aim of your prayer—namely, that God will make his life a blessed one. E. Stanley Jones puts it like this: "Every time the name of the person you dislike is mentioned, breathe a prayer for that person. You beat down rising resentments by a barrage of prayer. Make this a life habit, so that it does not become an issue each time."

If there is someone whom you dislike, and the mention of his name is like a pin sticking into your peace of mind, then the way out of your discomfort lies right here. Pray for him. Picture him as being in the presence of Christ, and see him set free from the meanness which caused him to wrong you; then let this Lord work his magic with him and make him the kind of man he was meant to be. I know not why it is, but I do know what it does; the proper kind of prayer is a practical step to get rid of resentment. You cannot pray for a person and continue to hate him to save your life.

III

There is a third word which our Lord has for us here—"do good to those who hate you." First, love your enemies, in the sense of desiring their welfare. Second, pray for them. And finally, do good to them.

If you take that word about "doing good" and look at it in the light of the life of the man who gave it to us, it will mean two things. It will mean, first, the offering of forgiveness to those against whom resentment is held. On his cross our Lord prayed for the forgiveness of those who had wronged him; and it goes without saying that what he asked his Father to do, he had already done himself.

When someone remonstrated with Lincoln that he had forgiven an enemy, he replied, "Our business is to get rid of our enemies, isn't it? Well, I got rid of this one by turning him into a friend through forgiveness."

A man walked fifty miles to beg George Washington to spare the life of a soldier sentenced for neglect of duty. "I'm sorry I cannot grant the request for your friend's pardon," said Washington. The man replied,

"He is not my friend; I suppose I do not have a worse enemy living." Washington looked surprised and said,

"Surely you are not pleading for your enemy?"

"Yes," said the man.

"Then," said Washington, "I will grant the pardon." The spirit of the man, says J. W. Brougher, so affected the soldier that he was changed into a friend.

That is the heart of the gospel: God the Father betting the life of the Son on the transforming power of forgiveness. If you really like to gamble, here is a place to play for high stakes: forgive your enemy and tell him so, then watch the magic work.

But "doing good" means more than a willingness to forgive; it means just what it says: *doing good*. Stanley Jones has reminded us that there are three levels of life and every man must decide for himself where he will pitch his tent. The first is returning evil for good, which is the demonic level. The second is returning evil for evil, which is the human, legal level. The third is returning good for evil, which is the divine level. You cannot read the New Testament, unless you have a tremendous blind spot, without seeing that the man who names the name of Christ is called to live on this highest level. In this very passage which gives us our text, Jesus says that the Christian will not demand an eye for an eye, but will turn the other cheek. And the Apostle, in his letter to the Romans, puts the matter in an unforgettable fashion: "Beloved, never avenge yourselves, but leave it to the wrath of God; for it is written, 'Vengeance is mine, I will repay, says the Lord.' No, 'If your enemy is hungry, feed him; if he is thirsty, give him drink; for by so doing you will heap burning coals upon his head.' Do not be overcome by evil, but overcome evil with good." (R.S.V.)

In the home where I grew up there were three brothers close enough together in age always to be getting in one another's hair. The doctrine we lived by was not that we were our brother's keeper but our brother's tormentor; and I'm sure our parents needed no theological proof of original sin. I remember one night at the supper table one brother had pulled a Dennis-the-Menace trick on another and the other was all set to retaliate. At that point our grandmother, who lived with us and who also lived with her Bible, spoke up. "Son," she said, "instead of paying him back, butter his biscuit for him and you will heap coals of fire on his head." In those days our kitchen still had a stove which cooked with wood, and the next thing we knew the maid appeared in the door with a small shovel piled high with coals out of the stove. That incident has imprinted this passage on my mind so that I shall never forget it.

But what does it mean? It is a quotation from Proverbs and it seems to mean this. Instead of paying back a bad turn with a bad turn, pay back a bad turn with a good turn. Such action will make the other ashamed; will burn like a fire to awaken his conscience, and will lead him to repentance. That kind of revenge will get rid of your enemy by turning him into a friend.

Professor Sorokin of Harvard is a sociologist interested in how people can best get along with each other. He has recently been given funds for the establishment of an Institute for Research into Creative Altruism. In his study of human relations he has discovered that love is the most powerful force, and he wants to find out why and how it works.

In our Christian faith we have not so much a definition as a demonstration. Once upon a time a group of men put to death another on a cross; instead of crying out for revenge he cried out to God: "Forgive them, for they know not what they do."

Such creative altruism has been working its wonders ever since. One of them concerns an old man who lived in the city of Alexandria in the early days of Christianity and was a devout believer. One day he was being tormented by a group of younger people who were unbelievers, and they mocked him and made fun of his religion. In their scorn, they hurled at him this question: What miracles has your Christ shown? This is what the old man quietly said: "He wrought this miracle, that I should endure the injuries which you heap upon me without losing my tranquility of mind, and should be ready to endure even greater injuries for love of him, if you were to proceed to inflict them." The story does not tell whether they became his friends, but the chances are that they did because love is always creative.

Donald Miller of Union Seminary in Richmond has written a book called *Fire in Thy Mouth*. What makes the book distinctive is the meaning which he gives to a sermon: "True preaching," he says, "is an extension of the Incarnation into the contemporary moment, the transfiguring of the Cross and the Resurrection from ancient facts of a remote past into living realities of the present. A sermon is an act wherein the crucified, risen Lord personally confronts men either to save or to judge them." Preaching, then, is not merely the repetition of words. It is a part of the redemptive deed of God performed by Christ on the cross, and by means of which that deed is repeated in the lives of men and women.

Would that the words on this written page might be a true sermon, that the same Christ who spoke them might step out from behind them and set us free from our resentments. To that end I bid you: "Love your enemies, do good to those that hate you, bless those that curse you, and pray for those that abuse you." (R.S.V.)

What About Faith
and Health?

"And he said to her, 'Daughter, your faith has made you well.' "
—*Mark 5:34 (R.S.V.)*

ANYONE WHO READS IN THE FIELD OF RELIGIOUS LITERATURE IS AWARE of the new interest in the relation between Christian faith and healing. Recently, I counted on my shelves thirty-five books on the life and teachings of Jesus. They are standard works written by recognized authors over the past fifty years; and in only one of them, and that a recent one, was there a chapter on the healing ministry of Jesus.

Yet a recent selection of the Religious Book Club is a volume written by Dr. Wade H. Boggs, Jr., titled *Faith Healing and the Christian Faith*. Several years ago a British minister named Leslie Weatherhead published a book called *Psychology, Religion, and Healing*. It is a major work of five hundred pages. Moreover, within the last three years four of our denominations have appointed committees to study the question of the relation of faith and healing. These are the Church of England, and the Presbyterian Churches of Scotland, South Africa, and the United States.

There are several reasons for this renewal of interest. First of all, there is the fundamental human desire for good health. All of us wish strongly to be well, and we are interested in anything which can promote good health. Secondly, there is the wide popularity of the faith healers, and the notoriety they have achieved through television. Finally, there is the new science called psychosomatic medicine, which is teaching us things we did not know about the close connection between the body and the mind, and which is making more reasonable to us the spiritual basis of good health.

65

As Christians we take the Bible as our source book on matters of faith and our theme has to do with Jesus and healing. We choose for our study one of the well-known cures which he wrought. One day a woman who had been sick for twelve years and who had gone from one doctor to another, sought him out. She had heard he could heal people, and with the desperation of a person who felt he was her last hope, she pushed through the crowd and touched his clothes. She was cured at once, and when Jesus turned around and looked at her he said, "Daughter, your faith has made you well." (R.S.V.) As we look at that picture there are several facts it suggests.

I

For one thing, the woman was healed. If the case stood by itself, and if you have a natural tendency to doubt, you might with real reason question the validity of the cure. But this case does not stand by itself. The gospel writers record at least nineteen incidents of this nature, and the maladies suffered by the patients range all the way from hemorrhage, as in this case, to fever, skin diseases, blindness, dumbness, lameness, and withered limbs. If you believe the Bible at all, you cannot doubt the fact that Jesus healed people.

That reminds us of the fact that Jesus made healing one of the major parts of his ministry. Along with teaching and preaching, healing was one of his major activities. Why did he heal? Some think he worked these miracles to impress people with his power and to prove that he was the Son of God. They look upon these wonders he wrought as "signs" by means of which he drew attention to himself and authenticated his claim to be divine. But such an idea goes strictly against the record. So far from desiring to call attention to himself, he very often instructed the person healed to say nothing about it; and sometimes when this part of his work began to take up too much of his time, he would leave one place and go to another so that he might have a chance to teach as well as heal. Moreover, some of his followers possessed this healing power, too, and they could not claim it as proof of divinity.

It makes better sense, I think, to say that the cures which Jesus performed were not so much signs as to who he was, as a revelation of his compassion. He healed people because, when he saw them suffer, he wanted to help them. It is much safer to put it that way, for two reasons. First of all, if our faith in Jesus' divinity rested upon his ability to work miracles of healing, and then we learned enough of the laws of health to perform the same cures, which more and more we are doing, then the grounds for our faith in his divinity would be gone. Secondly, if we find in his works not so much signs of something supernatural as indications of his helpfulness to people, then these cures give us guidance in our attempt to follow him with true fidelity.

For example: If Jesus healed because of his compassion for the needs of people; and if the church is, as it has been called, the "extension of the Incarnation," then the church is under obligation to provide as well as it can for the healing of the sick in hospitals and through the development of medical science.

II

The first thing we notice about the woman who was sick is that Jesus healed her. The second thing we notice is that he said to her, "Your faith has made you well." That fact leads us to say that faith has its part in all healing.

Sometimes it works directly, as in the case of this woman. Here is a sick person with whom the doctors failed, and yet who was healed by Jesus on the basis of her faith alone. Does that kind of thing happen today? I believe that it does sometimes. There seem to be some individuals who possess a peculiar ability to serve as instruments through whom the healing power can be passed on to others. Dr. Boggs, after a long and careful examination, puts it like this: "Most students of the faith-healing movement are not inclined to deny that some cures are authentic." Such a statement may stretch your credulity somewhat; but you will also be surprised to find the *British Medical Journal* saying a thing like this: "No tissue of the human body is wholly removed from the influence of the spirit." If that be true, and if faith and prayer are activities of the spirit, then all tissues of the body are within reach of their influence.

Shall we then as Christians dispense with all doctors and rely wholly upon the faith healers? By no means, because God heals indirectly with the skill of doctors as well as directly by faith. Every honest doctor will tell you that he does not cure the patient. All he does is to remove the cause of the illness and give the power of healing a chance to do its work. It was a doctor who said long ago, "I dressed his wound, but God healed him." And the doctor himself would be the first to tell you that he would be powerless without the power of healing which comes from God. It is only because he has gone to school and learned the laws of health and healing, and therefore knows how to meet the conditions of those laws, that he is able to heal. Leslie D. Weatherhead, a Christian minister who, so far as I know, is our ablest authority on the power of faith, says this: "Jesus Christ has more in common with a modern surgeon than with a modern faith healer."

Yet healing by doctors is not without the element of faith. It is written of Jesus that in a certain place he could perform no mighty work because of the unbelief of the people. The same is true of our doctors and of their work. There is no medical cure without faith. The doctor has to have faith in his medicine and in his instruments. The patient has to have faith in his doctor and in his doctor's faith. There was a great deal being said a few years back about the unwisdom of giving up the family physician who treated all our ills in favor of a specialist for this ailment and another specialist for that one. The point was that much of the effectiveness of the doctor's ability to cure lay in the confidence which the patient had in his doctor, a kind of confidence which was built up through friendship; and confidence is but another word for faith.

So the antithesis between the doctor and the faith healer does not hold water. It is just a question as to which one merits the greater confidence. As for me, I will take the doctor, because I think he knows more about his business and, therefore, is better able to mediate the healing which God can provide.

But suppose the doctor tries and fails. Suppose he comes to you and says: "I have done all I can for your child, and now it's up to God." Can you pray with any confidence that God might work directly? I think you can, because all healing comes from God, and faith and prayer in your case might be the very thing needed.

As a matter of fact, more and more Protestant clergymen are recognizing the resources for healing in faith and are making them available to people. The National Council of Churches sent out a questionnaire on this subject and 34 per cent of those answering said that they had attempted spiritual healing. They reported cures which included cancer and heart disease, and said that all cures had been verified by doctors. Theodore Ferris, of Trinity Episcopal Church in Boston, puts it like this: "We may reach the Source of healing power directly by prayer . . . or we may reach it indirectly . . . through medicine and surgery. . . . Why use one when you might use both?" "Our faith is neither in pills nor prayer. It is in God who may use both pills *and* prayer as channels of his healing power."

III

Thus far we have learned two things from the woman who was sick. The first is that Jesus healed her, and the second is that it was by her faith that she was made well. That leads us to the question: Will God always heal us if only we have enough faith?

The faith healers say Yes. All sickness, they claim, is caused by sin, and Jesus came to save us from sin and its consequences. Therefore, if we have enough faith we can always be healed; and if we are not, then something is wrong with our faith. Can such a statement be verified in the Bible? I think not.

When you go back to the Bible you find two facts, and both of them must be taken into account if you are to be realistic. The first is that God is active on our behalf in the healing of our bodies. Jesus was the Son of God and was known as the Great Physician, and you cannot believe anything other than that he was acting in line with the will of God in performing his cures. Furthermore, God created these bodies of ours and when you look at their recuperative powers, by means of which our doctors are able to do their work, you can believe nothing else than that they belong to us only by virtue of the good will of God. God is active in us and for us on behalf of health.

There is another fact, also: Jesus did not heal all the people who came to him. In one place we are told that, "He laid his hands on every one of them and healed them"; but our best scholars tell us that the verb translated "healed" means that he treated them. Furthermore, Mark tells us that in Capernaum *"all* who were sick" were brought to him; but he only says that of these Jesus healed *"many* who were sick." (R.S.V.) At the pool of Bethesda, you remember, there was a "multitude of invalids, blind, lame, and paralyzed." Yet Jesus healed only one of these. Moreover, you will find that no miracle was performed to cure Timothy's stomach disorder, and that Paul had a thorn in the flesh which stayed with him all his life. You cannot say that these men lacked faith in the least.

So then you have two facts. First of all, God is active on behalf of our health; and secondly, there are some good people who are not healed. In order to achieve a faith which is realistic, you must make a place for both facts; and such a faith I believe is possible.

It goes on to say that God wants us to have abundant life. When I am sick it gives me courage to know that God wants me to get well as much as I want the same thing for a child of mine. But while he wants me to have a healthy body, there is something else that he wants more; namely, that I grow strong in character and learn to be a little more like his Son. Sometimes he cannot give us both things at the same time. If health has to be sacrificed in order to grow a bigger soul, as happened with Paul, then that is the way it is, and I will have to learn to live with that fact. But I need not face it alone; for my faith tells me that even when God does not give me the power to get well, he will give me the power to meet my disability and transcend it and make it count for the better thing. That is what Paul means when he says: "We know that in everything God works for good with those who love him, who are called according to his purpose."

I went one day to see a man in the hospital. He was sick and the doctors had not been able to locate the cause. He was there to take some tests, the results of which he was then awaiting. When I rose to leave I said, "Well, I hope your news will be good news." I will never forget his answer. "To me," he said, "there is no bad news; for whatever comes is by God's providence, and that is good."

I think I know what he meant, and had he put it into words it would go something like this: "I want to be well and God in his wisdom can and may give me the power to get well; I will live for that and I will work for that. But if God in his wisdom does not make me well, I know he will give me the power to handle anything that comes to me with grace and serenity. Together he and I will work for the victory that is his will for me. My faith is not in a God who will always do what I want him to do, but my faith is in a God so great that he will enable me to do whatever he wants me to do."

That is a faith which takes account of all the facts; and I am certain that the Christ who drank to its last bitter dregs the cup of the Cross, will give to it his blessing.

How Can I Learn
to Grow Up?

"We are to grow up in every way into him who is the head,
into Christ."—*Eph. 4:15* (*R.S.V.*)

THERE CAN BE LITTLE DOUBT THAT MUCH OF THE UNHAPPINESS
which we encounter as individuals and as families stems from a
failure of some adults to grow up. Time and again some wife who
has come to talk about trouble in her marriage sums up the
case by saying: "My husband is still just a child in so many
ways." There are some characteristics of childhood which are
attractive in children, but when they persist across the years they
are like sand in the machinery of human relations.

It is not strange, therefore, that our Christian faith speaks
to this need, and so we find the Apostle writing to the members
of the church at Ephesus and saying this: "We are to grow up in
every way into him who is the head, into Christ."

I

Let us get into our truth by noting, first of all, what it means
to grow up. In one sense it is easy to grow up. All we need to do
is stay around long enough, get enough years under our belt, and
we who were boys and girls thirty or forty years ago are now
men and women. But you know, of course, that there are plenty
of people who are adults physically and yet are children
emotionally. The kind of growing up of which we speak is of a
more significant sort.

The new translations of the New Testament are a big help in
understanding Paul's meaning. There is a phrase in the same
paragraph with our text which the King James translators
rendered "perfect man." You find it in the sentence which goes
like this: "Till we all come in the unity of faith, and of the

knowledge of the Son of God, unto a perfect man." Another translation makes it read a "full-grown man." Then Dr. Phillips comes along and puts it like this: "Until the time comes when, in the unity of common faith and common knowledge of the Son of God, we arrive at real maturity." So that to grow up means to arrive at real maturity.

Now that word rang a bell in my mind. It reminded me that a few years ago we were reading a book called *The Mature Mind*. It is written by Harry A. Overstreet, one of our better-known students of human nature; and when I went back to the book, I discovered that he and the Apostle were in agreement. Paul tells us that our business is to grow up. Dr. Overstreet puts it like this: "The business of man is to mature: to mature psychologically, to mature along the line of what is unique in him and what he healthily shares with his fellows, and to continue the maturing process throughout his life."

I found furthermore that he has an entire chapter on the "Criteria of Maturity," and he listed certain tests by means of which you can check on your own life and see whether or not you are growing up. The first of these is being unself-centered "The human being," says Dr. Overstreet, "is born self-centered. . . . One of the most important phases of maturing is that of growth from self-centering to an understanding of relationship with others . . . . A person is not mature until he has both an ability and a willingness to see himself as one among others."

A childish jingle goes like this:

> I had a little tea party
>   This afternoon at three
> 'Twas very small—three guests in all—
>   Just I, Myself, and Me

Myself ate up the sandwiches,
While I drank up the tea,
'Twas also I who ate the pie,
And passed the cake to me.[1]

While such self-centeredness is somewhat more normal in children, because they are born that way, yet it is a mark of immaturity in grownups and when you stop to think about what it will do to ruin a friendship and spoil a marriage and mar happiness in later years, you see how important it is to help the child in your home or in yourself to grow out of it. So, one of the marks of maturity is unself-centeredness.

A second, according to Dr. Overstreet, is a sense of responsibility. "The human being," he says, "is born irresponsible. He did not choose to enter the human scene; and for a long time after his entrance he is helpless to do anything about it. Yet if we hear a grown man justify his lack of responsible participation in that scene by saying that, after all, he didn't ask to be born, we can set him down as immature."

One of the joys of childhood is the right to be carefree; yet the adult who indulges that freedom too far has failed to grow up: the wife who wishes the advantages of marriage but who resents the work necessary in running a home and rearing a family; the husband who wants a home but who resents the support of the family as an imposition; the college student who accepts the opportunity of an education but rebels against the discipline of study; the citizen who enjoys the freedom of democracy but who will not take the trouble to vote or share in civic enterprises; the church member who considers his duty done when he comes and sits and listens, but refuses to accept assignments in the

[1] Jessica Nelson North MacDonald, "The Three Guests." Used by permission.

church's work. The playboy who inherits a good living and shirks his share of the world's serious work is well-named, for while he may be fifty years old, he is still a boy. One of the marks of maturity, says the man who knows, is a sense of responsibility for doing one's part.

A third mark of maturity, according to the expert, is an integrated life. The word integer means a whole, and to integrate is to bring together into wholeness. "The child," says Dr. Overstreet, "is born to a world of particulars. He has to mature into a world of wholes."

You have noticed, I am sure, that a child's interest cannot be held by any one thing for long at a time. You give him some blocks to play with and he is fascinated for a while; but before long he is bored with them and wants something else to do. His interest lacks integration. The Apostle mentions this characteristic in the passage which gives us our text. He pleads with his readers in Ephesus that they achieve a mature manhood. "So that we may no longer be children, tossed to and fro, and carried about by every wind of doctrine." (R.S.V.)

One such child of forty years came to my study one day. It was about her marriage, she said. She and her husband had not been getting on and she felt terribly imposed upon. She had talked with her friends. One said this, and one said that, and she was all mixed up. She didn't know whether to leave her husband or try to stick it out. What she needed to do was to grow up—to get hold of a principle that would tell her what was the right thing to do and then do it, and forget the conflicting advice of different individuals. Her trouble was that, like a child, she was "tossed to and fro, and carried about by every wind" of advice.

So then there are three criteria of maturity: a life that is grown up will be unself-centered; it will have a sense of responsibility for doing its part; and it will be able to fit together into a whole the various parts of this jigsaw puzzle which is human experience.

II

Then there is a second truth in our text. Not only does it tell us that we are to grow up, but it suggests the means by which we can achieve our maturity. "We are to grow up," says Paul, "in every way into him who is the head, into Christ." We are talking about the business of helping people grow up. I am convinced that our own happiness as individuals and the well-being of our world depends upon our achieving this maturity. I am further convinced that our Christian faith offers what we need in meeting this goal. As I sit in observation upon my own experience, and as I seek to help those who come to my office for counsel, I am more and more persuaded that the more we grow into Christ, the more we grow into real maturity.

Take, for example, this business of self-centeredness. Our Lord recognized how self-defeating it is for individual happiness and how dangerous it is for the world's well-being. He taught that expansion of the self into other selves which can overcome the dangers of self-centeredness. Granted that self-regard is one of the strongest impulses of our nature. All of us are interested in ourselves and it would be dishonest to deny it. Jesus is altogether levelheaded here. What he says is this: "Love thy neighbor as thyself." Love yourself well, but do not stop there; go on and love your neighbor as you love yourself. "He that findeth his life shall lose it"—begin by centering yourself on yourself and you will end by hating the self you are centered on. A man who is all wrapped up in himself makes a mighty small package, so small in fact that he will be disgusted with it. He that findeth his life shall lose it. And he that loseth his life for my sake shall find it."

Here is a six-year-old child who was sent to a private school. He had been there only a few weeks when he had a so-called "nervous breakdown." They took him to the doctors and their explanation was that he had been spoiled in his own home, and for the first time in his life he could not be the center of the stage and have things his own way.

The same explanation would fit many adult cases. If you are interested in the future well-being of the boys and girls who are growing up in your home; if you are eager that they achieve a healthy-mindedness which is a guarantee against going to pieces, then you will see to it that Christ gets hold of them to the extent that they are lifted out of their self-centeredness.

Take again this business of a sense of responsibility. I know of nothing better calculated to save a life from being irresponsible than the gospel of Jesus Christ. Look once again at the way in which he responded to life. At the age of twelve his parents missed him from their company. When they went to look for him and found him in the temple and began to ask him why he hadn't come along, he said this: "Did you not know that I must be in my Father's house?" (R.S.V.) And once again, when he started out on his life's business he put it like this: "I am come . . . not to do mine own will, but the will of him that sent me." (R.S.V.) He has a sense of responsibility to a higher will, and when we are willing to learn from him in this regard, we will have the same.

Take it in the matter of vocation. So often we begin at the wrong end. We say to a boy, "What do you want to do when you grow up?" We should be much better Christians and far kinder to our young friend if we put it like this: "God has a job for you to do and, if you will listen, he will tell you what it is; when he tells you, then do it; only then will you reach your deepest happiness and your highest achievement." There is no substitute in the world for the will of God to give a man a sense of responsibility. The same goes for husbands and wives in the home, and students in college, and citizens in a community.

Finally, take this business of a life which is integrated into a wholeness which finds meaning in all the parts. You see how important is this factor when you look at one of the expressions we use to describe a patient who is mentally sick; we say he has "gone to pieces." The reason for his illness is that he lacks an integrating principle which can pull him together and fit the pieces into a pattern which has meaning.

The secret of integration is a purpose which commands and unifies all the interests and energies of your life and there are various kinds of aims and loyalties which have this power. For Napoleon it was personal ambition; you can look at his life and see how it was pulled together and made subservient to this one aim. Yet the purpose which has the greatest power to integrate is to be found in our Christian faith. It is the greatest because it takes in the whole range of human experience. For example, one of the most disintegrating of all things is trouble. Illness lays you low, or physical handicap robs you of your hopes, or death strikes in your home. You say, "Why should this happen to me?" You shake your fist in the face of heaven, and you are miserable because you cannot fit this fact of trouble into your scheme of things, and more and more you go to pieces.

Yet, when you come to think of it, Christ himself was not without trouble. While yet in his thirties his own family thought him crazy, his friends deserted him, and his own nation put him to death. Paul was the same. He had a thorn and the time came when he was beaten with stripes, and stoned to the point of being left for dead. Surely this man had enough trouble to make him go to pieces; but he did not because he was a mature person. This maturity came from his faith that "all things work together for good," for the only final "good," which is that we conform to the image of the Son of God.

I have recently been reading the autobiography of Harry Emerson Fosdick. He says that one day he went to see a woman who had gone blind. She had been an active person and blindness would go hard with her. But she had also been a golfer and what she said to Dr. Fosdick was this: "I'm in a sandtrap now: but watch me take my niblick of faith and get out." There was a person who had arrived at real maturity. She did not go to pieces because she had learned to integrate all the facts, even those she did not like, into a wholeness which gave them new meaning.

Here then is your task: as men and women we are to grow up into a real maturity as integrated, responsible, expanding persons. We have at hand in our Christian faith the answer to our need, for we grow up best when we grow up into Christ.

What Can I Do
with Life?

"For to me to live is Christ."—*Phil. 1:21*

A RECENT BOOK BY A WRITER NAMED HAROLD WALKER IS CALLED
Power to Manage Yourself. That title suggests the fact that each
of us has on his hands a thing called life and must do something
with it.

You may like it, or you may not. You may curse the day you
were born and resent the fact that your parents did not consult
your wishes in the matter. You may say with Job: "I should
have been as though I had not been; I should have been carried
from the womb to the grave." Be that as it may, you have no
choice now whether to be or not to be. The philosophers tell
us that reality is that which must be taken account of. The reality
of the present situation is that you have this thing called life
on your hands, and your only choice is what you will do with it.
There are in general four different choices open to you.

I

For one thing, some people decide to deal with life by running
away from it. A man named Jonah in the Bible was given a job
by God but he ran away from it; he boarded a ship and set off in
the opposite direction. Another man, in the story told by Jesus,
was given a talent and told to put it to work. The other two men
in the story did as they were told, but this poor fellow went out
and dug a hole in the ground and buried his talent. He ran away
from his responsibility. This method of dealing with life is so
common that our students of human nature have a name for it.
They explain much of our conduct as being what they call an
"escape mechanism." Unable to face the demands which reality
makes upon us, some of us find ways of retreating into escapism.

For example, the teacher calls to say that your child is sick at school and wants you to come for him. Sure enough, he has a bone fide case of nausea. When the same thing happens several times, you begin to investigate and you discover that some unpleasantness has developed between the child and his teacher or some fellow pupil, and he wants to escape from it. His body co-operates with his mind by making him sick. Once you discover the cause and find a solution, the illness does not recur. In many cases of chronic illness among adults the cause is nothing more than an evasion of responsibility—this business of running away from life.

This fact explains in large measure much of the drinking that goes on about us. A British officer in India, warned that he was drinking too heavily, lifted his glass and said, "My friend, this is the swiftest road out of India." Someone asked a man in Manchester, England, why he drank liquor and his reply was: "It's the shortest way out of Manchester." A doctor named Stracher states the truth in scientific form: "Alcohol is used as an escape from the responsibilities and burdens of mature emotional life and its decisions. It provides wish-fulfillment." If you do not like the world you live in, then you run away from it and build up an unreal world for the time being. If you are unhappy, you seem to be happy. If you are frustrated, you seem to be free. If you are weak, you seem to be strong. You are like the mouse that found a cask of wine dripping in the cellar. He took one taste and began to feel his muscles, he took two tastes and stood up on his hind legs, faced the world and said, "Now let the cat come on!"

The same fact explains many of the divorces granted by our courts. Someone says that a good sailor will not jump overboard in the first squall on the sea of matrimony, but many of us are not good sailors. We run away from the responsibilities of the marriage we have made and seek an escape in divorce. Much of our mental illness has the same cause. A visitor at a mental hospital saw a workman hauling materials for a new building. Among them was a patient with a wheelbarrow, but turned upside down. When the visitor asked him why he had it upside down, he replied: "Do you think I'm crazy? If I had it turned up, they would fill it." That answer no doubt explained the reason why he was there. He had run away so much from the responsibility of pulling his load that he found permanent residence in the unreal world of insanity. Of course the ultimate in the search for escape is suicide; and the 100,000 people who attempt suicide in this country every year indicates how strong is this tendency to run away from life.

The trouble is, it never works very well. Ask Jonah. Ask the man who dug a hole in the ground and buried his talent. If you are looking for something to do with your life, don't run away from it.

II

There are other people who try a different method. Instead of trying to run away from life, they choose to run along with it. When in Rome they do as the Romans do. One night the men in a certain church were serving their own supper. They took over the kitchen and prepared the meal and set the tables and served the food. The janitor was there and everybody was his boss. He was sent on one errand, and before he was able to get that done, some other man had commandeered his services. He was going round in circles. One man noticed what was going on and he said to the janitor, "If it's this bad with the men, what do you do when the women are in charge?" The poor fellow replied, "I just put my mind in neutral and go where I'm pushed." Those who run along with life put their minds in netural and go where they are pushed.

Here was Simon Peter, for example. His Lord had been arrested and taken before the high priest. Simon followed along and found himself in the court of the high priest. Someone there recognized his speech and remembered having seen him at the time of the arrest and said to him, "Weren't you with the Galilean in the Garden?" Three times they put the question to him. Simon had been a sailor and he knew how to curse. He let out an oath and said, "I do not know the man." Simon did not run away when the soldiers came; let that be said to his credit. He stayed by and was within seeing distance of his Lord; but for the time being he was running along with the crowd. When he was put on the spot he lacked the courage to stand up and acknowledge his discipleship.

Someone has well remarked that for the first three hundred years of its life the story of the Christian Church could be written under the title, "The Church in the World," but that since the time Constantine legalized Christianity and baptized the crowds en masse, the title of the story would have to be turned round to read, "The World in the Church." There is indeed too much of the world in the church when many Christians deal with life by running along with it. Cheating is the accepted thing in some schools and colleges. So-called Christian students go along with the practice because everybody's doing it. I am amazed at the lack of conscience about gambling in the form of betting on football games and golf matches by professing Christians. Many a drinker has become an alcoholic because he lacked the backbone to ask for ginger ale in place of a highball at a social gathering. You would be amazed, could you sit in a minister's conference room, to see how many so-called good people have fallen for this Hollywood nonsense that if you don't love your wife any more, you have the right to cast her aside. There is absolutely nothing in the vow to make marriage dependent upon mere feeling. And, unfortunately, there are those who are guided by the principle that the fact that so many people practice sexual promiscuity makes it right.

The word of God to the Church today, as in the first century, runs on this wise: "Be not conformed to this world: but be ye transformed by the renewing of your mind." Perhaps you will want to begin now to take inventory and mark with an "x" the spot where you will draw the line on some things because you are beginning to see the light. God made this world and he put something in it called the moral law; you cannot break that law to save your life, but you can be broken by it.

Some years ago a senator was standing in a room in the Capitol in Washington when a picture fell from the wall and struck him on the head. Someone rushed up and asked what he could do. The senator had a sense of humor and replied: "Go in there where the Senate is meeting and get the law of gravitation repealed." In like manner a gypsy one day went to Confession and the priest asked if he knew the Ten Commandments. The gypsy said: "It's this way, Father. I was going to learn them but I heard tell they were going to do away with them."

The Ten Commandments are like the law of gravitation. They are woven into the warp and woof of this universe and you can't repeal them to save your life. Life was made to work God's way, and sin is plain suicide.

III

There is a third way in which some people deal with life. Instead of running away from it or along with it, they decide they will run it.

Sometimes you find one of these people as the father in a home. He is a perfect Hitler. When he says "scat," he will tell you he means scat. His word is law, and it is based neither on intelligence nor on reason nor on love. Sometimes you find this person in business. I remember hearing about the head of a company who put it like this: "What is a board of directors for, if not to do as I say?" Sometimes you find him in the church. I knew a minister once who used to say this: "The best kind of Board in a church is one which never meets." He wanted to run things his way.

Too often that attitude carries over into life in general. This man will tell you that wherever he sits is the head of the table. His time is his own and he will do with it what he pleases. His money is his own and no preacher, even though he quotes the Bible, is going to tell him what to do with it. His freedom is his own, and he will sow his wild oats where and when and how he pleases. His friends are his own, and what is a friend but to serve your own advantage? He is a self-made man who worships his maker. His life is his own, and he will run it as it suits him.

The trouble is, however, that too often he runs it into the ground. The ultimate sin is for a man to put himself in the place of God; and when a man tries to run his life, without reference to God, he is riding for a fall.

IV

That suggests the fourth and final method of dealing with life. Instead of running away from it, or running along with it, or seeking to run it, the best answer I know is to put it into Christ's hands and let him run it for you. That is what Paul means in the text: "For me to live is Christ." Instead of running away from it, I will be able to stand up to it because he stands by me. Instead of running along with it, I will go only as far as he can go with me. Instead of running it into the ground, I will make him my quarterback and let him call the signals. Forgetting the things which are behind, and reaching forth unto those which are before, I make this my goal: to me to live is for Christ to live over again in me.

E. Stanley Jones says that in one of his informal meetings a man stood up and said: "I've been running my own life; I've been like a person learning to drive a car, flooding the carburetor, choking up things, starting and stopping. Now I've moved over and let Christ take the wheel. It's different now."

You can see why. He said, "I'm come that they may have life and have it to the full." (Moffatt.) That sentence comes from the gospel of John in which the word "life" is equivalent to the word "salvation" in the other three gospels. The word salvation is defined like this: "freedom from dangers menacing to life, and the consequent placing of life in circumstances favorable for its highest development." The purpose of Christ for your life is that you be set free from all the things which harm you, and that you be given all the help you need to reach your fullest and finest and best. I have never seen a home in which Christ was made a member of the family where things were not better for all concerned. Have you? I have never seen a life put into Christ's hands with permission to run it, where there was any desire to go back to the old way. Have you? As one man put it in our Couples' Forum one evening: "I've tried it both ways: Christ's and the devil's, and I'll take Christ's."

One night I was meeting with a group of members of Alcoholics Anonymous. One of the men referred to the four paradoxes of AA, and the first one was this: you have to surrender in order to win. There are many similarities between the teachings of AA and the teachings of our Christian faith, and this is one of them: you have to surrender in order to win. If you want to be master of yourself, you must first of all be mastered by a Master.

We come right back to the place where we began. You have on your hands a thing called life and you must do something with it. Stop trying to run away from it, or to run along with it, or to run it by yourself. You have tried one or all of those three and have gotten nowhere. Why not try Paul's way of putting your life into Christ's hands and letting him call the signals? You can take my word for it: once you give your life to him, he will give it back to you better than it's ever been before.

What Does It Mean
to Be Born Again?

"Jesus answered and said unto him, Verily, verily, I say unto thee,
Except a man be born again [from above] he cannot see the
kingdom of God."—*John 3:3*

WHEN THE EVANGELIST BILLY GRAHAM SPOKE IN OUR CITY, HE
referred so often to "born again Christians" that many persons
were left wondering what he meant. One man who was deeply
moved by the meetings brought this question to me. "What does
it mean to be 'born again'?" It is a good question.

Any talk on this theme takes you back immediately to
John 3:3. There our Lord receives a visitor named Nicodemus.
It is somewhat out of the ordinary, because this man is a member
of the "Supreme Court"; yet there was something about this young
teacher which even VIP's couldn't resist. Whenever gentlemen
meet, compliments pass, and Nicodemus is a Chesterfield. He
opens the conversation by saying, "Rabbi, we know you are a
teacher come from God; for no one can do these signs that you
do, unless God is with him." (R.S.V.) But the answer he re-
ceived set him back on his heels. "Jesus answered and said unto
him, Verily, verily, I say unto thee, Except a man be born again,
he cannot see the kingdom of God."

It was as if a church officer of mature years might walk up to
a young man of about thirty who had just come to town as a
new minister and say to him, "My friend, I believe in giving
folks their flowers while they are still living. You must have the
goods, for no man can fill a church Sunday after Sunday, as
you've been doing, unless he's got something on the ball and the
blessing of God is with him." And without waiting to thank
the man for his compliment, the minister should change the

subject abruptly and say to him, "But that's not the point—the point is, have you been born anew?"

It rather swept Nicodemus off his feet, and pretty soon he found himself sitting and listening to the greatest teacher of them all as he spoke of a subject made fascinating by its mystery.

I

The first thing we learn, as we join that audience under the Syrian sky, is the utter necessity of this business of being born again. They tell a story about Whistler: once a friend of the artist's called on him to advise concerning the hanging of a painting which had been purchased a short while before in Paris. He complained to Whistler that he could not make the painting fit the room. "Man," said Whistler, "you're beginning at the wrong end. You can't make that painting fit the room. You will have to make the room fit the painting."

You are a fortunate man indeed if ever you succeeded in getting into the Christian life without meeting with that fatal mistake of trying to make the painting fit the room. Here is the room of your life, and here is the painting of the Christian way. Try hanging it without changing the room. Try turning the other cheek, and forgiving seventy times, and going the second mile, and loving your enemies without some help outside yourself, the help of God. It is like trying to wear a shoe that does not fit your foot—it hurts. The way out is not to cramp your toes into space that is too small for them—the only remedy is to get a new shoe. The only way for a man to wear the Christian life with any ease and pleasure at all is not to jam the teachings of Jesus into a life that doesn't fit them. It is to get a new life. I wonder if most of the quarrels we have with Jesus, the thing which makes his way so hard, do not come from the fact that we are trying to do what he says without first having caught his spirit. We are trying to make the painting fit the room.

It is a necessity of the first water. "That which is born of the flesh is flesh," he said to Nicodemus. Somewhere in your ancestry something happened that blacked out the image of God. "Adam begat a son in his own likeness, after his image"—not the image of God. And that blackout has been passed on from generation to generation. "I was shapen in iniquity," said David. He does not mean that the process of procreation by which he was born is in itself evil; he meant that through that process he inherited a bias toward evil, and so does every son of man.

If you think that a libel on human nature, ask yourself if the way of Christ comes naturally. You talk to your friend and he says, "Why should I forgive that fellow? He deliberately stuck a knife in my back. Why should I forgive him?" Self-preservation is the first law of life for him. The Christian way does not come natural to a man. You will never get him to forgive until he is willing to say, "God, for Christ's sake, has forgiven me, and wants me to forgive every man against whom I have aught."

That which is born of the flesh is flesh, and no amount of dolling it up and decking it out with Christian morals will ever suffice. Have you ever tried praying and reading the Bible and tithing and going to church, only to throw it off again and again as a yoke that galls and burns, until one day you catch the spirit of Christ and for the first time have a good time being a Christian? That is what it means to be born again, and it does not come natural to a man. So, says Jesus, the thing of which we speak is an absolute necessity: Ye *must* be born anew.

II

Move on now and notice, in the second place, that Jesus speaks not only of the necessity of this experience; he promises furthermore its *possibility*. "That which is born of the Spirit is spirit," he says.

A certain newspaper which prided itself upon the fact that it seldom made a mistake, once reported the death of a citizen who was very much alive. He came into the editor's office later in the day to protest. "I'm sorry," said the editor, "but if this paper says you are dead, then you are dead." The only compromise he would make, after long discussion, was to print the man's name in the birth notices the next morning. It is possible for a man to read in the record of his daily experience the notice of his death after the flesh, and his birth after the spirit.

If you ask me how it happens, I have to tell you I do not know. I cannot explain either how God makes something out of nothing; the mystery of creation is no less mystifying than the mystery of re-creation; the mystery of birth is no less a mystery than rebirth. I cannot explain, either, the truth that darts like a flash of lightning into the soul of man and changes his whole life. Yet here is Paul, and here is Augustine, and here is Francis of Assisi, and here is—well, you can fill in the names you know.

And yet, though I cannot explain it, I can tell you how it pictures itself to my mind. I have read this verse times without number and it meant nothing to me: "except a man be born again." I must confess I was like Nicodemus. I didn't see how a man could enter a second time into his mother's womb and be born again. Then one day I happened to read it in another translation and instead of saying, "Ye must be born again" it said, "Ye must be born anew." That small difference in words made a large difference in understanding. I noticed a marking over the word "anew" which referred the reader to the margin and there I found something even better. There I was told that instead of reading this verse "Ye must be born again" I could read it "Ye must be born from above."

Right away that turned on a light which made this word shine with rich meaning. E. Stanley Jones points out that there are five kingdoms, representing different stages of being. At the bottom is the mineral kingdom and above that the plant kingdom, then the animal kingdom, above that the kingdom of man, and at the very top, above the human, is the kingdom of God. You and I then, as men and women, stand between two kingdoms: the animal kingdom below us and the kingdom of God above us. We are akin to the animals, through this body of flesh. We are akin to God through the spirit which he breathed into this body. Having this double kinship, we can be "born"; we can draw the impulses which control our living from beneath or from above us.

Some people seem to be born entirely from below. They are more like animals than they are like either man or God. They eat like pigs, drink like camels, drive like road hogs, show-off like peacocks, deceive like foxes, and lord it over everybody else like lions. Self-preservation is the first law of their natures, and self-sacrifice is altogether foreign to their make-up. It is not a pretty phrase, but the Apostle describes them to a "T" when he says their "God is their belly." They are born from below. Their idea of heaven is wine, women, and song; and their motto is, "Let us eat, drink, and be merry." They live for what they can get out of life, never coming within seeing distance of the fact that it is more fun giving than getting. They are born and they live entirely from below.

Then there are those persons who are born from above. There is a spirit in them which is different from the spirit of the jungle.

They are more like God than like a growling grizzly bear. They have found a thrill in something besides eating and drinking and lusting. They find their lift for living not in bending the elbow but in bending the knees. They are still human beings—they live in the flesh; yet the difference is they do not live for the flesh. Spirit rides herd over the flesh. You will find their description in the thirteenth chapter of I Corinthians, and you can see their picture in a portrait of Christ. Born from above—that is what it means to be born again.

I was talking with a friend once about this picture of our truth and he said, "Yes, I see it now; like a deep sea diver, who is kept alive by the oxygen which is piped down to him from above, so is the person who is born of the spirit: from above comes the divine oxygen which is the breath of life."

III

There is only one more thing that remains to be said. You will get the proof of this experience not by explaining the mystery of it but seeing the results of it. If you want to know whether this thing happened in your life, or the life of someone else, look not at the roots but at the fruits. "Marvel not that I said unto thee, Ye must be born again. The wind bloweth where it listeth, and thou hearest the sound thereof, but canst not tell whence it cometh or whither it goeth: so is every one that is born of the Spirit."

I think the two men must have been sitting out in the open. The record says it was at night, and you can see them there, trying to get a breath of fresh air on the flat roof of one of those Syrian houses. A soft breeze blows up while Jesus is speaking. "Nicodemus, do you see those leaves moving in the tree there?"

"Yes."

"What makes them move?"

"The wind."

"Well, where does that wind come from?"

"I don't know."

"Where does it go from there?"

"I can't say."

"Just so. The wind blows where it wills: you hear the sound and see the leaves swaying, but you cannot tell where it comes from or whither it goes." So you cannot write a handbook on the Holy Spirit and say he will come in this way and no other. The work of the Spirit of God in the soul of a man cannot be mapped and charted and graphed. You know that God has visited that man when you see the footprints of God in his life.

I say it in all reverence, but I have often shied off from the folks who talk too much about being born again. It seems to make them queer and to take from them that sane balance and common sense which you find about the life of Jesus. I once heard a man say that he did not want any of the second blessing. He said he would take all he could get of the third and fourth and fifth, but that there was something about the second blessing which did funny things to folks; it made them fanatics. But a fanatic is not a person who has too much religion; it is a man who has too little sense. You need never be afraid of getting too much of the spirit of God, because the fruit of the Spirit, says Paul, "is love, joy, peace, patience, kindness, goodness, faithfulness, gentleness, self-control." If you want to know whether or not you have been born from above, you can use this check-list. You will find it in the letter to the Galatians, the fifth chapter, and the twenty-second verse, R.S.V.

A friend told me that once he found himself with an evening on his hands between trains in a city away from home. He thought of going to a movie but he remembered that an old gentleman, a friend and contemporary of his father's, lived there. His father had died some years before, and he thought it would be like a visit with his father to go out and see the old friend. So he telephoned, told the old gentleman who he was, and asked if he might come out. He took a cab to the address and rang the doorbell. The old gentleman answered the door and swung it open. Before shaking hands or speaking any word of greeting, he stood back and looked his guest up and down. My friend said he began to wonder if his suit were not pressed or his hair not combed, or just what was the matter. He said he had never been subjected to such close examination. Finally the old man shook his hand and said, "Well, I was just looking to see if there is anything of your father in you."

I've thought a lot about that: "just wanted to see if there's anything of your father in you." "That which is born of the spirit is spirit." He that is born from above will have something of the life that comes from above.

So we come back to the point where we started: How can I know that I have been born again? Well, it's really very simple. Sit down and close your eyes and see yourself in the mirror of memory, and find out if there's anything of your Father in you.

What Makes Sin Sinful?

"And the son said unto him, Father, I have sinned against heaven, and in thy sight, and am no more worthy to be called thy son."—*Luke 15:21*

HARRY EMERSON FOSDICK WRITES THAT WHEN HE WAS A BOY, HIS father said to his mother as he left the house one Saturday morning, "Tell Harry that he can cut the grass today, if he feels like it." Then after a few steps he turned and added, "Tell him that he had better feel like it."

Some of us sometimes think of God as a person who has issued certain orders, and has said to us concerning them, "You can obey them if you like—but you had better feel like it."

These orders seem to be simply arbitrary commands, just some queer notions of his, designed to take the fun out of life, and altogether unrelated to the business of living. The sinfulness of sin therefore to our minds is simply our failure to observe certain rules which are queer notions of God. We resent being told if you do it this way you will go to heaven, but if you do it the other way you will go to hell. Somewhat as if a father might draw a line across his backyard, irrespective of where the flower beds lay, and say to his son: It is all right for you to play on the right side of the line, but if you get over on the left side I'm going to whip you.

As long as we think of the sinfulness of sin as disobedience to rules set up for flimsy reasons, and punishment for sin as the penalty for such disobedience, we shall continue to hold a grudge against God as a despot who wields the whip hand just because he can.

If we can rise to that insight which sees the commands of God, not as the queer notions of a psychopathic dictator, but as the signposts set up by a friend to keep us on the only road which leads to our fullest life, then we shall not so much begrudge the rules which fence us in, as we shall be grateful for the trouble they can save us. It is a red-letter day in your life when you see that a thing is not wrong because God forbids it, but God forbids it because it is wrong; and that what makes it wrong is that it hurts you.

I

Perhaps the best way to turn a spotlight on that fact is to put it this way: we are punished not so much for our sins as by them. When the boy whom we call the Prodigal went back home he said to his father: "Father, I have sinned, . . . and am no more worthy to be called thy son." No one was punishing him for his failures; he was punishing himself by them. Out in the far country he had allowed himself to sink to the level of a beast. He had destroyed within himself, by his manner of living there, the quality of life as a son, and so he came back saying: "I am no more worthy to be called a son—let me be your servant." He was punished not so much for as by his sins.

That fact is true because of the way things are in this world. Some of you are acquainted with the Westminster Shorter Catechism and its answer to the question, What is sin? "Sin," it says, "is any want of conformity unto, or transgression of, the law of God." The Catechism goes on to tell us that the law of God is summed up in the Ten Commandments; and you know those rules about not stealing or killing, or committing adultery. Now what makes these things wrong? Are they wrong simply because a God who wants to take the fun out of life says they are; or is there a deeper, more fundamental reason?

In order to get the answer to that question you have to see that the world we live in is built on what is called a moral foundation. That means that it rewards what is right and it punishes what is wrong. Suppose a bullet, as it leaves the barrel of your rifle, says to itself: "I don't care anything for gravitation. I will keep on going as long as I like." Yet for all its speed, it will not beat out gravitation in the end. Gravitation never lets go. It always hangs on, because that is the way things are in this world.

What the law of gravitation is in the physical world, so are the commandments in the moral world. They have not been set up by God to take the fun out of life; they have rather been given by God to keep us from hurting ourselves. "I had thought that faithful marriage was hell, but what have I been living in?" said a disillusioned young woman who had revolted. She found that that law about adultery was written into the commandments because it was first of all written into life. "Even if you do succeed in escaping the police, there is something inside yourself you can't get away from," said a thief who came back to give himself up. He found that the law about stealing was written into the commandments because it was first of all written into life. Look, there goes Judas. He is getting ready to hang himself. Stop him! "Judas, why in the world are you doing such a thing?" "I can't help it," he says; "I have murdered a man." The law against murder is written into the commandments because it is first of all written into life.

Any man who breaks a commandment is doing what Judas did: he is hanging himself. That is true because sin is suicide. It is self-destruction. That is what makes sin sinful; not in the first place because it violates the laws of God, but because it violates the laws of life. The laws of life are the laws of God. "I am come," says Jesus, "to bring you life." Your doctor will tell you that the right thing is always the healthy thing. Of course it is, because that is the way the world is made: it rewards what is right. It's true the other way too: the wrong thing is always the unhealthy thing. Of course it is, because that is the way the world is made: it always punishes the wrong thing. I sometimes think that we preachers would get further if we pointed out that sin was not so much wrong as stupid, because that is what it is. It is definitely not smart. It is "dumb" as the teen-agers put it. Look at the prodigal: he went out to see life, and what he found was death. Look around among your acquaintances: they count themselves out one by one, as the chickens come home to roost. Sin is anything that hurts a person; and therefore what makes sin sinful is the injury which it brings to people.

II

That injury will be felt by the person who sins. The prodigal tells us that first of all: he had lowered himself in his own estimation from a son to a servant. His sin had cost him his money, and it had cost him his self-respect. He had been hurt and that was what made his sin sinful.

You probably wonder why preachers talk so much against liquor. As a boy I used to wonder the same thing. I have heard some of them rant like fanatics, and it seemed to me they were being unreasonable. Now I understand, because in the last thirty years I have seen some of the things which liquor does to people. Dr. Robert V. Seliger, who is a psychiatrist at Johns Hopkins, put it much better than I can say it. He claims that "men of distinction may drink to extinction."

He said something else which interested me. He said that "drinking alcoholic beverages is not sinful but unwise—because it can kill you, it can make you 'tell off the boss,' it can cause sex indiscretions in young ladies, it is costly, and it makes a driver a menace." Not sinful, but unwise! Here you have the old popular idea that what makes sin sinful is the breaking of some arbitrary law set up by some God who loves to be a kill-joy. Why can't a man see that sin is sinful just because it is unwise—because it hurts the person who indulges in it?

That is the reason why worry is a sin: because it gives you stomach ulcers and brings on heart attacks. That is the reason hatred and resentment are sins: because they make you sick and send you to a doctor. That is the reason self-centeredness is a sin: because it cuts you off from your friends and makes you sick of yourself.

A man who worked much with taxes and little with the rules of grammar heard someone speak of "syntax" and he said, "My goodness, is there a tax on that too?" Well, ask the man who knows—and who doesn't? A young man who was going to New York to live once asked the late S. Parkes Cadman this question: "Doctor, can I lead a good Christian life in New York City on $15 a week?" "My boy," said Dr. Cadman, "that's all you can do." Sin costs—and once again you can ask the man who knows.

III

You can ask the people to whom that man means something— they know too. When the prodigal reached home he said, "Father, I have sinned in thy sight." Do you think he needed to tell his father that? Don't you think his father knew? What of all the sleepless nights he spent, wondering where his boy was, and all the gray hairs put in his head by not knowing whether his boy was alive or dead? What of the piercing pain he felt whenever he saw that empty chair at the table? What makes sin sinful is that it hurts—not only the man himself but other people too.

That is one big trouble with sin. If it were an individual matter only, if a man could reach out and take hold of all the consequences of his sin, and bring them to bear upon himself alone, he might go on his merry way without thinking more about it.

101

"I'll pay the price—I'll consume my own smoke." But that's the trouble; it is not a private affair.

That is true because of the way life is made. We are all tied together in a bundle of life. We are not like flowers planted in flower pots and lined up in a row, each separate from the others. We are like the threads of a piece of cloth, all woven and interwoven with each other. We are husbands and wives, brothers and sisters, mothers and fathers and friends. As Paul would put it, we are members one of another. Let one member of a family catch a cold, and the chances are it will run through the family. Let a young man take his turn at the far country—and his father stoops under the weight on his shoulders. His mother's hair turns white and her happiness black. His brothers and sisters get the cold shivers every time they hear the rattling of the skeleton in the closet. Eve ate her apple, and the daughters of Eve have been paying for it ever since. Achan stole the spoils of war, and forty of his tribesmen paid with their lives. Jonah boarded the ship and became a Jonah for all on board. The sins of the fathers, as the Bible puts it, are visited upon the children unto the third and unto the fourth generation.

That is the trouble with sin. What makes it sinful is that it hurts—it hurts the person himself and all those whose lives are tied to his.

IV

It hurts God too. When the prodigal came back he said, "Father, I have sinned against heaven." Not only against himself, so that he was no more worthy to be called a son; not only against his father, and all members of his family; but against heaven, and the God of heaven.

Every sin is a sin against God; not simply against a God who, as an impersonal moral order, sets up these laws which break a man when he tries to break them, but a God who has a heart inside him. God is not a fiend who says, "I told you so," when you bring home the shattered pieces of a life broken against the rock of righteousness, and who hardly looks up from reading his paper. He is rather like a father who says, "O my son Absolom, my son, my son Absolom! would I had died for thee." (A.S.V.) He is like that schoolmaster who, when two of his students broke a rule, began to fast, and refused to eat anything until they came to him in penitence and with the promise they would mend their mistake. He took it upon himself.

Have you ever seen the pain on the face of a parent whose son or daughter has been hurt playing with this thing called sin? I have, and I tell you it is a sight you can never forget. I think now of a mother who died a thousand deaths as she watched her son throwing his life away. God, says Jesus, is like a mother, like a father. He feels it too. If you want to know what your sin does to God, look at the cross! There it is, in plain sight, for all to see. That is what sin does to God. Before ever again you take off for the far country, shut your eyes and see this man nailed to a tree, and ask yourself this: Is it worth it—is this little fun worth crucifying afresh the Son of God?

V

Strange as it may seem, it is just this in God which has done more than anything else to bring men to their senses so that they decide to have done with the stupidity of this thing called sin. They have felt themselves the penalty for their sins and they have seen the blight put upon other lives than their own. But when they catch sight of a God who doesn't scold them—or pick them up and spank them—but who takes their sins upon himself, and who goes the second mile of giving his Son to die for them;

103

they can't stand that. It puts penitence into their hearts, and tears into their eyes.

The late Dr. Eliot, former president of Harvard, said that the strongest appeal he was ever able to bring to bear on wayward boys was in making clear to them how much they had been sacrificed for and how much their failure would mean to those who cared. That is what we have in the Cross: look at that picture, and there you can take the measure of how much you have been sacrificed for and how much your failure will mean to the God who cares.

In the church school at Riverside, in New York, a class of fourteen-year-olds was discussing the question why Christ had to die, and one of the boys put it like this: "Jesus," he said, "saw a lot of good in this world, and he didn't like the way it was being pushed around. Somebody had to take the rap, and he took it."

"Somebody had to take the rap, and he took it." Will it be for nothing that he took the rap, as far as you are concerned? Or will you see here something of what makes sin sinful, and have done with this stupid thing forever?

God is waiting now to hear how you will make answer.

What Does the Bible
Say About Drinking?

"Don't get your stimulus from wine [for there is always the danger of excessive drinking], but let the Spirit stimulate your souls."—*Eph. 5:18 (Phillips)*

OUR THEME HAS TO DO WITH THE DRINKING PROBLEM AND WE ENTER it by noting two facts. The first has to do with the size of the problem. There are one hundred fifteen million people in our country of drinking age and sixty-seven million of them use alcoholic beverages to some extent. Seven million of these—one out of every ten—get into serious trouble through their use of liquor. Yet every one of these seven million has relatives and friends, and so it is estimated that twenty-five or thirty million people in America are affected by problem drinking. The national liquor bill is nine billion dollars a year, eight times as much as is spent on education and twenty times as much as is given to churches. The disturbing fact is that the problem is getting larger: drinking is up 33 per cent since 1940, and in some states arrests for drunken driving increased 100 per cent.

In addition to the size of the problem, there is the difficulty of knowing one's duty. To drink or not to drink? is a serious question with many people. There is the young person just beginning to go to parties where alcoholic beverages are served, and there is the normal adult Christian whose conscience is uneasy about a social custom which is so generally followed. There is the action of some churches which calls for voluntary abstinence, and yet there is the miracle of Jesus who turned water into wine, and the word of Paul to Timothy advising the use of wine. In view of the difficulty of decision, where can you go to find an answer to the drinking problem which is both intelligent and Christian?

For the believer in Christ, the Bible is regarded as the final rule of faith and practice. As I bring this question to its pages, it seems to me the Bible says three things.

I

The first thing it has to say is that the drinking habit is harmful. "Wine is a mocker, strong drink is raging: and whosoever is deceived thereby is not wise." "Who has woe?" asks the author of Proverbs; "Who has sorrow? Who has strife? Who has complaining? Who has wounds without cause? . . . Those who tarry long over wine, those who go to try mixed wine. Do not look at wine when it is red, when it sparkles in the cup and goes down smoothly. At the last it bites like a serpent, and stings like an adder. Your eyes will see strange things, and your mind utter perverse things. You will be like one who lies down in the midst of the sea." (R.S.V.) The Bible says that drinking is like a snake that bites, and the difficulty is that its harmful sting is felt by so many innocent people.

In my files there is a letter which came from a radio listener in Texas some months ago: "Five years ago my youngest daughter with whom I lived was killed instantly along with her husband and four others in an auto wreck, and all because of a drunken driver who wanted to get ahead in heavy traffic; and since then I have so many doubts and fears and often wonder if I have lost my faith in the goodness of God." Then she asked, "Why don't you ministers do and preach more against this terrible liquor business?" When I learned that two hundred thousand of the one million auto deaths in our country were due to drunken driving, it made me realize that was a good question.

In my files also is a picture of a twenty-six-year-old man as he was booked for the murder of a young woman found in a pool of her own blood on the floor of a room in a hotel several summers ago. The reason I kept the clipping was that it gave this explanation of the crime. "The thing which I did," said the young man, "I had no intention whatsoever of doing; and if I had not been under the influence of whiskey and beer as I was, and in my right mind, it would never have happened."

"Booze is the mother of crime," says Judge William M. Gemmill of the Chicago Municipal Court. "I have tried an army of 50,000 human derelicts, most of whom were booze soaked." The distiller asked the judge, "Did you ever try one of my fine brands?" "No," said the judge, "but I have tried plenty of men who did."

On the economic side Benson Landis tells us that bills chargeable to drinking go like this: potential wage losses, four hundred thirty-two million dollars; crime, one hundred eighty-eight million; accidents, eighty-nine million; hospital care, thirty-one million; and maintenance of drunken persons in local jails, twenty-five million. When these figures are added to the original cost of the liquor, the total bill is a staggering ten million dollars.

When you turn from the economic to the human side, the picture is even more dismal. A Federal Committee says that "the abuse of drink is directly or indirectly responsible for more than 20 per cent of divorces, 25 per cent of insanity, 37 per cent of poverty, 47 per cent of child misery, and more than 50 per cent of crime."

As a growing boy attending church it seemed to me that the preachers were fanatics about drinking. I often wondered why they went to extremes in their denunciation of alcohol. Now I know. When you care for the well-being of people, and when you see what it does to wreck their lives, it makes you hate it with an everlasting hatred. The Bible is right. Alcohol is a snake that bites, and in its sting is destruction.

II

The second thing you find when you bring this problem to the Bible is that nowhere does it set up a rule which says that you must not drink. This Book has much to say against drunkenness, but there is not a single verse I know which prohibits your taking a drink. Moreover, there is the miracle of Jesus in which he turned water into wine for the guests at a wedding feast, and there is the word of Paul to Timothy about taking a little wine for his health. Does that mean then that as a social or moderate drinker you have the approval of the Bible for your habit? That question must be answered by saying that the Bible does not set up detailed rules for living, but suggests certain principles which have to be formed on the basis of facts.

One of these facts is that the liquor industry depends for its life upon the social drinker. It is the fifty-eight million moderate drinkers, and not the seven million problem drinkers, who support it. It would go out of business if it depended upon the small minority of compulsive drinkers.

The second fact is that it is the moderate drinker who is the dangerous driver. If your friend has passed out you can put him on the back seat and not under the wheel. But the man with only a few drinks under his belt insists on driving. Experiments in Denmark prove that two beers, which yield only 4 per cent alcoholic content in the blood will affect certain driving skills as much as 40 per cent. Dr. Richard Cabot, Professor of Clinical Medicine at Harvard, summarizes the situation like this: "The excessive drinker doesn't usually drive when drunk. Moderation is thus more dangerous than excessive drinking as the cause of automobile accidents. There is no hope, therefore, of decreasing motor accidents by working for moderation. Only abstinence can make us safe." The moderate drinker does not reel when he walks, but he kills when he drives.

The third fact is that the social drinker creates the problem drinker. The more drinking, the more drunkards is a fact of life. Studies reveal that 6 per cent of all moderate drinkers turn into compulsive alcoholics. The experts say there is no way of telling whether you will land in the 6 per cent or stay in the 94. When you give a cocktail party and there are forty guests present, two of them will be ruined by alcohol.

The fourth fact is that beverage alcohol is a different substance now from what it was in biblical days. The distillation of hard liquor was not known until the thirteenth century, and therefore what the Bible says about drinking must be considered in the light of that truth.

The fifth fact is that churches like the Baptist, Methodist, and Presbyterian have called upon their members to abstain from the manufacture, consumption, and distribution of alcoholic drinks. Again and again they have said that voluntary abstinence is the ideal for the Christian. This action does not state a rule which lays down a condition of membership. You can still disagree with that judgment and be a member of one of these churches in good and regular standing. But you have to do it knowing that the considered opinion of your church is against you.

When we go back to the Bible for guidance on the question of moderate drinking, we do not find any specific prohibition. Neither, however, do we find that the Bible in so many words says that slavery or dueling or child labor is wrong. Yet as men gradually came to understand the meaning of God's will for human lives, they banished these evils from the earth. So it is that we will have to judge the problem of drinking on the basis of certain principles. If we believe the drinking habit makes people kinder to each other, if it blesses homes and increases capacity for abundant living, if it makes it easier for people to do the will of God, then we must be all for it. But if its total effect is against the things that God intends for men, then we have to be against it.

III

Move on now and notice a third truth. When you set the drinking problem down alongside the Bible you discover what is called the law of Christian conscience. Paul states it for us in the First Letter to the Corinthians.

In the city of Corinth there were many temples where idols were set up to false gods. The worship of some of these idols included the sacrifice of animals. After an animal had been killed, sometimes the meat was cooked and served for food. The question as to whether or not it was right to eat such meat which had been offered to idols was a burning question among the Christians. Paul seems to indicate that if he had only himself to consider, he could go on eating such food without any scruples; but if his example led someone else who did have such scruples to follow suit, then he was bringing injury upon another. "For," he says, "if any one sees you . . . at table in an idol's temple, might he not be encouraged, if his conscience is weak, to eat food offered to idols. And so by your [example] this weak man is destroyed . . . Thus, sinning against your brethren and wounding their conscience when it is weak, you sin against Christ." (R.S.V.) And then he goes on to lay down this rule for himself: "Therefore, if food is a cause of my brother's falling, I will never eat meat, lest I cause my brother to fall."

Here, it seems to me, is the closet parallel to be found in the Bible to the man who says that he has been drinking for years and it hasn't done him any harm and he doesn't see why he should stop. Paul says that eating meat offered to idols did not injure him in the least; but he went on to say that it was wrong for him if someone else was harmed by his example. And then he lays down this rule for us: "It is wrong for anyone to make others fall by what he eats; it is right not to eat meat or *drink wine* or do anything that makes your brother stumble." (Rom. 14:20-21 R.S.V.)

That statement begins to take on meaning for us when you look at it in the light of the reasons why people drink. People drink for three reasons: because they can't help it, because they like the taste or its effects, and because other people are drinking. The third reason accounts for one half of all the drinking that is done. That means that thirty-three million people drink because of social pressure. Therefore, the social drinker, by force of example, is responsible for wrecking the lives of 165,000 confirmed alcoholics.

There is another word in the Bible which deserves to be set alongside that of Paul. It comes from Jesus and what it says is this: "Whoever causes one of these little ones who believe in me to sin, it would be better for him to have a great millstone fastened round his neck and to be drowned in the depth of the sea." (R.S.V.) That sounds like a harsh statement, but it comes from the lips of our Lord himself, and you cannot get away from its meaning. The man or woman who encourages a young person to drink or who makes it difficult for him not to drink, carries a heavy responsibility. That includes the liquor interests with their extensive advertising campaigns. It includes the "boss" who throws a liquor party for the force. It includes the hostesses who do not serve anything except beverage alcohol. And it includes parents.

For example, the Yale study called *Drinking in College* gives

111

those of us who are parents something to think about. It says that where both parents drink, 92 per cent of the men and 83 per cent of the women students drink; that where one parent drinks, 83 per cent of the men and 54 per cent of the women students follow the example; but where both parents abstain the proportion of those who drink falls to 58 per cent of the men and 23 per cent of the women. The authors sum up the case in this manner: "These data suggest that parental example is a factor of major significance in drinking by young people."

And the same thing holds good for church members and officers. "Social pressure," which accounts for one half of the drinking that is done, remember, is but another name for the power of example. That puts a heavy responsibility upon the churches, for many of you who are its members are the social leaders of your communities. "Whoever causes one of these little ones who believe in me to sin, it were better for him . . ."

It was my pleasure once to attend a birthday dinner in honor of the late Senator Cameron Morrison of North Carolina, who conscientiously practiced voluntary abstinence. A person of perception who was present paid him this tribute: "Others will think of your contributions to public life," she said, "but I honor you, Sir, for something else. As the first citizen of Charlotte, your example of abstinence has contributed immeasurably to the sobriety of our people."

So we come back to the place where we began: the problem of personal decision is a difficult one.

As you face your own decision, I give you this word from the apostle Paul: "Don't get your stimulus from wine [for there is always the danger of excessive drinking], but let the Spirit stimulate your souls."

What Does It Mean
to Imitate Christ?

"Christ . . . left you an example, and you must be following his
footsteps."—*I Pet. 2:21* (*Moffatt*)

IN THE YEAR 1380 A BOY BY THE NAME OF THOMAS HAMMERLEIN
was born in the Prussian town of Kempen on the Rhine, some
forty miles north of Cologne. At the age of twenty he entered the
monastery of Mount St. Agnes, and for the next seventy years
lived the quiet life of a monk: copying manuscripts, writing, and
performing the routine of the monastic life. In his school his
family name was forgotten and he was called by the town from
which he came: Thomas from Kempen. We know him today as
Thomas à Kempis, and the only reason we remember him is
that he wrote a book. It is small, as books go, occupying only
170 pages in the Harvard Classics; but it ranks with Bunyan's
Pilgrim's Progress and the *Confessions* of Augustine as one of
the three top writings on Christian devotion. The name of this
little book is *The Imitation of Christ*.

Thomas à Kempis describes for us here the business in which
every Christian is engaged. We are to be imitators of Christ.
We can read our Bibles and pray our prayers and recite our creeds
and attend our services; but all such exercises are beside the point
if they do not lead to what Kempis calls the imitation of Christ.
Peter puts the truth into a few words for us in the verse: "For
Christ left you an example," he says, "and you must follow his
footsteps." What does that mean?

I

Merely to say, however, that the main business of the Christian
is to imitate Christ does not settle the matter for the man who is
in earnest. The chances are it will unsettle him, for it is too vague

an answer. Suppose you should hear about Christ for the first time today, and should be so laid hold upon by him that you decided to give him your allegiance. You are told that your handbook in the Christian life is the four gospels. Here is the picture of his life; now, copy it for yourself. You would soon get lost amid a welter of details. I wonder sometimes if we preachers are not often to blame for the unsatisfying religious experience of our people because we are so indefinite. We say, for example, that the duty of the Christian is the imitation of Christ, and then we stop there.

It would be more helpful, would it not, if we went further and examined and analyzed that life, separating it into its component parts, listing its basic elements, and then with these virtues in hand, created a design for living? In the Gospels, for example, we have a series of inimitable pen pictures of our Lord. We would not wish it otherwise. Emil Ludwig says somewhere that "the anecdote best defines the personality." What we know of the life of Jesus is the total impression made upon us by the recital of these incidents. Underlying all the actions of Jesus as described in these stories, there are certain guiding principles. If you could then take the stories of the temptation and the miracles and the teaching and suffering of Christ and analyze them, as a scientist breaks down a chemical compound into its elements, then you might be able to list—one, two, three—the virtues which it is ours to incarnate. Then you would have something practical. Then you would have a standard by which you could check yourself and test the progress you make with the passing days.

Fortunately for us that has been done by a great Christian. No less a man than Robert E. Speer has taken the trouble to reconstruct from the life and teachings of Jesus the four standards with regard to which he never allowed himself an exception, and with reference to which his life and his teaching are absolute and unyielding. As the scientist takes a beam of light and passes it through a prism to see it broken into its constituent colors, so does Dr. Speer pass the life and teachings of Jesus through the prism of his mind to get to the least common denominator of that character. Once we know his results we have a practical guide in the imitation of Christ, and the words of Peter take on definite meaning: "For Christ . . . left you an example, and you must be following his footsteps." What then is that example?

II

In the first place, the imitation of Christ demands the practice of purity at all times. You can see how absolute is this test when you apply it to Jesus in the form of a question: Was Jesus ever impure? From what we know of him, you cannot imagine that for a moment Jesus would show hospitality to an unclean thought or consider an impure act. His decision would be as definite and his action as final as his memorable words to Simon: "Get thee behind me, Satan." Here is something which is absolute and ultimate and the last word. "Blessed are the pure in heart." "If thy right eye causeth thee to stumble, pluck it out." (A.S.V.) "The wisdom that is from above is first pure." (R.S.V.) It is never right to be impure. It is never wrong to be clean. Purity of thought and speech and action is a sure test of the imitation of Christ.

If carried to its full meaning absolute purity would include victory over every sin; but in order to be definite and practical it can be pin-pointed at the place of sex. It is clear that many so-called Christians are substandard according to this test in their imitation of Christ. More than one young woman has come to my study for counseling and has brought with her this question: "The man in my life asks the full enjoyment of love even before we are married: how should I answer him?" The only answer I know is that as Christians we have a certain standard. That standard has been set by God for our own good, and we flout it only at our peril. As far back as the Ten Commandments there is something about not committing adultery, and in the New Testament it is written: "This is the will of God . . . that ye should abstain from fornication." Popular writers may report incontinency among a high percentage of unmarried people, but that has nothing to do with the question. Your business is the imitation of Christ. He has left you an example and you must follow in his steps. His example was one of absolute purity.

III

In the second place, the imitation of Christ demands honesty at all times. In the very next verse following the text Peter says: "No guile was found on his lips." (R.S.V.) The dictionary says that guile is an act of deceiving, and deception is dishonesty. Here then is another standard which is absolute. You can test its absoluteness by putting it in the form of a question: Was Jesus ever dishonest? No, says Peter, he was not. He was as honest as the day is long, and you bear witness to your recognition of that fact when your conscience takes you to task for lying or cheating or stealing. "Provide things honest in the sight of all men," writes Paul. Honesty, then, in intention, in speech, and in action is a sure test of the imitation of Christ.

Here is a word which has something to say to us. I remember in college a certain student who was something of a tinker with machinery. He opened the pay telephone placed in the dormitory and so manipulated the machinery that instead of keeping the money it was returned to the coin box. He then telephoned his girl friends in colleges many miles away, and his money was returned to him. He thought he was smart, but he was also dishonest. The manager of a telephone company recently told a college president that often he found in coin boxes a twenty-five cent piece with a hole in it and a string tied to it. The string was used to retrieve the coin, and sometimes the string broke. The manager of a hotel in a southern city gave out the information that within a year's time his hotel lost ten thousand towels, sixteen hundred sheets, six thousand pieces of flat silver, one-hundred all-wool blankets, twelve-hundred bathmats, two-hundred-fifty pillow cases, and one hundred cream pitchers.

Taking linen from a hotel and cheating a telephone company are not the only forms of dishonesty. From writing the translation of a Latin lesson in the margin to manipulating an income tax report to one's advantage, and all the way in between, there are subtle ways by which we fall short of this virtue. All betting and gambling are dishonest, because they attempt to get something for nothing. Most gossip is dishonest, because it usually embroiders the truth. Taking credit for ideas or achievements which do not belong to you; letting someone else suffer for your wrong deeds; sharp dealing in trade; lying about a child's age so that he might travel for a cheaper fare; quoting an author's words out of context for the purpose of criticism; mixing money accounts; telling only a part of the truth for the purpose of deceiving; and discussing personal confidences—all are forms of dishonesty.

The Bible opens with a picture of two people who believed a lie. The teller of that lie was rightly named, and the telling of that lie has wrought its misery upon men. Dishonesty in any form is always destructive, while honesty is more than the best policy. It is an absolute standard, and as such it is a part of the imitation of Christ.

IV

Our design for living does not stop with being pure and honest. It proceeds to virtues which are more demanding. It requires always the practice of kindness. Once more, you can test this standard by applying it to our Lord in the form of a question: Was Jesus ever unkind? The question answers itself. Here, then, is something which is ultimate.

The word which Jesus used most often is love: "Thou shalt love thy neighbor as thyself." But in order to keep love from stopping short at emotion, I prefer to define it on its positive side as everyday human kindness. It is going out of your way to help somebody. It is giving the cup of cold water. It is the good Samaritan lending a helping hand to the luckless traveler. It is the good turn of the Boy Scout. It is helping the old lady across the street, visiting a sick friend in the hospital, writing a letter to a lonely soul, fixing a tray of food and taking it next door. Someone says that you can take the word "Christ" and substitute it for the word "love" in the thirteenth chapter of First Corinthians and it will fit perfectly. Love is kind, says Paul; and Christ is kind; they do fit exactly. Make love to mean kindness and see how perfectly you can put the equality sign between love and Christ. They equal each other. So true is that fact that when Peter wanted to write the biography of our Lord in five little words he summed it up—"who went about doing good."

Once again, here is a word for us to take to heart. All too often our goodness is a negative thing. It is a painful avoidance of evil rather than a glad performance of kindness. We are more concerned about not doing the things that are wrong than we are to be sure to do the things that are right. Some soldiers were talking about a new man who had recently joined the company. "He is a queer fellow," one of them said. "He doesn't drink, he doesn't smoke, and he won't gamble." "Then," said another, "he must be a Christian." At best it is a left-handed compliment to judge Christianity by what it does not do. I like rather the thing that was said about Sir Henry Bartle Frere. He was a British nobleman and was expected for an engagement in a certain city. The chairman of the reception committee, never having seen him and wanting to know how he might recognize his guest at the railway station, was told: "If you see a tall gentleman helping somebody, that will be Sir Bartle Frere." What do you think it would mean to the heart of our Lord if it could always be said with truth, "If you see a man or a woman or a boy or girl helping somebody, that will be a Christian."

V

There is yet a fourth factor in the imitation of Christ. Dr. Speer calls it unselfishness, by which he means that mastery of self when self is tempted to sins of the heart like anger and resentment. I prefer to call it forgiveness. I save it for last because it seems to be the most difficult duty of all, and yet it is the one most Christlike. This is the thing Peter seems to have in mind above all others when he tells us that Christ has left us an example, and we should follow him. He says that if you do wrong and suffer for it and take it patiently, you do not deserve any credit. But if you do what is right and suffer for it and show patience, then you have God's approval. He proceeds to speak of the example left us by Christ who, "When he was reviled, he did not revile in return; when he suffered, he did not threaten; . . . By his wounds [patiently accepted and forgivingly borne] you have been healed." (R.S.V.)

119

Here then is a final factor which is ultimate and which can be tested by the question: Was Jesus ever unforgiving? Once again the question answers itself. In his teaching he told Peter he was to forgive his enemies not seven times but seventy times seven, which means without limit. And what he taught, he lived. When his enemies had arrested him unjustly and refused him a fair trial and nailed him to the cross, he did not shake his fist in their faces and cry out in anger that when he got back home to heaven he would get even with them. He forgave them and tried to find an excuse for them. "Father, forgive them; for they know not what they do."

Here again is something for us to go by. Self is so important to most of us that we build a standing army and wait for the chance to declare war on anyone who steps on our toes. It is always wrong to be unforgiving; it is always right to forgive. If you are serious about this business of the imitation of Christ you cannot harbor a grudge or nurse an injury. You will love your enemies, and do good to them that hate you, and pray for those who wrongfully use you. You will remember what Paul said: "Do not be overcome by evil, but overcome evil with good." (R.S.V.) If you wish to know what that means you can remember Henry Ward Beecher. They say that when Beecher lived in Brooklyn he had a neighbor who hated him cordially; but the preacher had a spirit so patiently forgiving that the man finally said this: "If you want a favor from Beecher, kick him."

Here then is a design for living: to be clean and kind and honest and forgiving. These qualities are not vague; they are as practical as the dollar in your pocket and as real as your neighbor next door. They are ultimate; beyond them you cannot go, and short of them you cannot stop. In the incarnation of them lies the imitation of Christ.

How Can I Be
Really Free?

"For wide is the gate, and broad is the way, that leadeth to destruction, and many are they that enter in thereby. For narrow is the gate, and straitened the way, that leadeth unto life, and few are they that find it."—*Matt 7:13-14* (*A.S.V.*)

OUR THOUGHT IN THIS CHAPTER TAKES ITS STARTING POINT IN THE fact that so many of us want to be free and yet go about finding freedom in the wrong way. As a young person, feeling that too long have we been tied down by the apron strings of a strict discipline and longing to get away from home so that we may kick up our heels and be free to live our own lives; as a man or woman stepping over into the dangerous forties, feeling we are not understood by our family and rebelling against a conventional morality which puts a stop sign at the gate which leads into greener pastures; we want to be free. We want release from the bonds which bind us to a galling servitude; and then when we kick over the traces and go out in search of that new freedom we find ourselves bound in the bonds of a more servile slavery. It all seems rather confusing.

A friend of mine who has a way of seeing into the nature of things makes a distinction between the two words *liberty* and *freedom* which might help to clear up the confusion. We have a way of using the two words as if they meant the same thing. However, they do not at all. While liberty is the power to choose either right or wrong, freedom is the consequence of making a right choice. His meaning will become clearer as we go along; but meanwhile, we note that our Lord puts the truth in a picture of the two ways: "For wide is the gate, and broad the way, that leadeth to destruction; narrow is the gate, and straitened the way, that leadeth unto life."

I

As we set these words up in front of us and begin to look at them, the first thing they say to us is this: while liberty is a gift, freedom is an achievement. As I stand in front of the wide gate and the narrow gate, I am at liberty to choose which one I shall enter; but from that point on my freedom in the future will depend upon which choice I make.

From this point of view it is interesting to recall that what the Declaration of Independence demands is that all men have "life, *liberty,* and the pursuit of happiness." It does not say freedom, but liberty—that is—the right of choice. Freedom is something else; freedom is a man's fullest opportunity to be and do his best. Such freedom is the consequence of a right choice, because it is the product of discipline.

For example, I remember how it worked out in my case in the matter of playing football in college. I possessed liberty in that regard. I could choose whether or not to go out for the team, and that power of choice was a gift. It cost me nothing. But suppose I had gone to the coach and said, "Coach, you can put me in the line-up for Saturday, but I don't think I'll be out for practice this week." You know what would have happened. I possessed liberty as soon as I hit the campus, but freedom to play? Well, you know that wasn't a gift but an achievement. An achievement which could be reached only through the narrow gate and straight way—the narrow gate of discipline. It meant the discipline of the training table—no cakes or pies or hot bread, nothing but toast from September until Thanksgiving. It meant the discipline of regular hours—bed at ten o'clock every night. It meant the discipline of hard practice every afternoon. Liberty was easy, but freedom was hard. Liberty was a gift, but freedom was an achievement. Liberty was the right to choose, but freedom came only as a consequence of right choice.

You can take this truth and set it down in the midst of your own experience and see what it has to say to you. Here you are a high school or a college student and you want to be free—free to lead your class and at the end of four years to serve as valedictorian. Well, you have liberty to choose, but you do not yet possess freedom to do so. Nobody can hand you that on a silver platter. It is something that has to be won. If you choose the broad road of movies every afternoon and evening, and dates and trips every week end, you will have to give up your freedom to lead your class. If you choose to enter the narrow gate, the gate of discipline, and to travel the straight road of concentrated application to work, then you might win your freedom.

Surely the musician knows this truth perhaps better than any of the rest of us. He wants to be free—free to become a concert or opera star. He is at liberty to choose which of the two gates he shall enter. If he chooses the wide gate, the gate of laxity in practice, and the broad road, the road of trying to eat his cake and have it too, he will lose his freedom. A friend of mine is studying now for the concert stage and his teacher said to him, "You have the voice but it will take work, and if I find you are not working I will drop you like a hot cake." Liberty is a gift, but freedom is an achievement. It is an achievement which must be reached by way of the narrow path of discipline, and the straight road of concentrated work.

Of course this truth reaches out beyond the individual to the universal. We all wish, of course, to be free to live in a world at peace. As people and as nations we have our liberty now. The last war is over and we have our choice. Freedom to have a world which is permanently at peace will not come so easily. It is not a gift but an achievement, a desperately difficult achievement, an achievement which each one of us must devoutly desire and earnestly seek to promote and continually pray for.

Dr. Leslie Weatherhead says he was staying once with a poet. "I said to him: 'It must be very wonderful to be able to write four perfect lines of poetry.' He said, 'Well, you are free to try.'" So am I, but should I try, I, like Dr. Weatherhead, would not want to show the real poet the result.

No, this thing of freedom is not the simple affair we sometimes supppose it to be. It is not a gift but an achievement. It is not to be had for the asking; it must needs be sought after with the whole heart. It will never be found through the wide gate of live-as-you-like or down the broad road of do-as-you-please. It will be reached only through the narrow gate of self-discipline and down the straight road of devoted loyalty.

II

As these words of our Lord stand up in front of us, let us walk around them and note this fact: once you enter the narrow gate the way becomes broader, and once you enter the wide gate the road becomes narrower.

At first thought one might suppose that such is the case for the simple reason that there is more room on one road, and less on the other. You will not find the way nearly so crowded if you enter by the narrow gate. "Few there be that find it," says Jesus. And we mean the same thing when we say that there is plenty of room at the top of any profession. But it is not simply the fact that the traffic is less pressing. It belongs to the nature of freedom that once you enter the narrow gate the road begins to broaden, and once you enter the wide gate the road begins to narrow.

"When I was a young man," says Dr. Albert Goodrich, "I taught in the ragged schools of London. On one Sunday I had this passage for my lesson. 'I say, teacher,' merrily sang one of those sharp ragged boys, 'it says, don't it, the way to the good is narrow and the way to the bad is wide?' 'Yes, it does,' I replied. 'I know that's true,' he said with a knowing wink; 'but,' he added, dropping his voice, 'is it fair? Oughtn't God have made them both the same width? He'd have given us, then, a fair chance.'"

Well, it is not that God wanted to load the dice against us and make things any harder for us; it is just that it belongs to the nature of things that anything worth while can be found only through the narrow gate. What we are doing now is to make that gate more inviting by coming face to face with the fact that once you enter the narrow gate the road begins to widen and once you enter the broad gate the road begins to narrow down.

Here are two friends whom I knew in theological school. They both wanted to be free—free to serve their generation to the top of their talents through the ministry. One of them chose the wide gate, the wide gate of a lazy, idle life, and by his middle year at school you could see the road begin to narrow down, so that by the time he reached his senior year the road ran out as he had to leave school and give up the ministry. The other man however chose the narrow gate. I had known him in college and I did not believe he had it in him. But when he reached theological school he buckled down. He showed a capacity for work he had never revealed before. He practiced a stern self-discipline, and every year his road grows wider, his freedom becomes larger, as church after church seeks his services.

Of course, you do not have to think very hard to see how this truth holds in another realm where freedom is more familiar to more of us. Here are two other men whom I knew in college. Both of them wanted to be free in later life—free to marry and settle down and have a home and children. One of them said he had been brought up in the straight and narrow, and when he listened to the boys talk of their exploits he felt rather like a sissy. He entered marriage through the narrow gate and now he has found his freedom—freedom to be the father of several fine children. But the other man, who desired such freedom just as genuinely as the first, chose the wide gate. He had his fling. He sowed his wild oats. But when he married he found that chickens do have a way of coming home to roost. Because he had chosen the wide gate the road had narrowed considerably: he had forfeited his freedom to be the father of the children he had wished.

Just exactly why one gate should seem narrow and the other wide I do not know, but I do know this: once you get on the inside, the narrow gate opens upon a broader way, and the wide gate upon a narrower road.

III

Walk once more round these words and take a look at them, and they will throw new light upon the real meaning of self-denial.

Have you ever stopped to consider how unreasonable we are in our conventional way of thinking about the discipline which goes under this name? When a preacher talks about the sacrificial life it is commonly understood to mean one thing only, the costliness of goodness. Our Lord said, did he not, "If any man come after me let him deny himself and take up his cross and follow me"? Surely, we say, the kind of life for which Christ stands costs heavily. That is self-sacrifice, we think, to choose the highest and pay its price. It costs so much to get into the narrow gate and it is so easy to get into the wide gate that we put one down as the way of self-denial and the other down as self-indulgence.

The truth of the matter is something else altogether. Everything we choose, whether good or bad, we pay for. The only difference is in when you pay for it. If you choose the narrow gate, you pay for what you want before you get it. If you choose the wide gate, you pay for what you want after you get it. If a man chooses the wide gate and the broad way of dissipation and promiscuity, we have a way of saying that he is living a life of self-indulgence. But when you stop to think about it, that is not self-indulgence but self-sacrifice. It is utterly impossible to choose between a life of self-indulgence and a life of self-sacrifice. All we can do is to choose between two kinds of sacrifice—giving up the worst to get the best, or giving up the best to get the worst. At the end of the road entered by the narrow gate stands Life, says Jesus; at the end of the road entered by the wide gate stands destruction. You can pay your money and take your choice— either way, you have to pay.

Now listen to a man who paid his money and took his choice: the choice of the narrow gate and the straight way. It is Dr. Fosdick speaking from the seventy side of the sixties:

I thank God now in my elder years that I did not make some sacrifices when I was young. I had to choose, as all you young people must, which should be my aim, a Christian home with its deep fidelities and satisfactions on one side, or on the other, a loose life of sensuality. Well, I chose! Long before I met the girl I married I wrote her a letter, in which I said that somewhere on earth I knew she was alive and waiting for me and that some day we would meet, and that in the meantime I was going to keep my fidelity to her as true as though she now were mine. You say that cost. Of course it cost! But now in retrospect, think what it would have cost had I

127

made the other choice, to have surrendered all the deep and sacred satisfactions of these lovely years for a mess of pottage! [1]

There are some of you readers who are impressed by Dr. Fosdick's words because you have proved their truth the hard way. When you were younger and had your choice, you chose the wide gate. You kicked over the traces and went out to sow your oats and have your fling and live as you liked. You wanted to be free. But ever since you've been finding out that you found not freedom but a prison: a prison of guilty memories, a prison of shameful waste of talent, a prison of a childless home, and a prison of thwarted dreams.

I believe you would offer this advice to those who are younger: My friend, if you are so fortunate as still to possess liberty, the power of choice over what to do with your life, consider: this thing called freedom is not easy, it is hard; it is not a gift, it is an achievement; it costs, yes, but it is worth all it costs. You can pay your money and take your choice—but either way you have to pay. And take it from me: it is so much more sensible to give up the low and get the high than to give up the high and take the low.

When men who have tried it both ways say the same thing, it must be so.

---

[1] Harry Emerson Fosdick, *On Being Fit to Live With* (New York: Harper & Brothers, 1946).